Generative Phonology Workbook

Generative Phonology Workbook

M. Stanley Whitley

The University
of Wisconsin Press

Published 1978

The University of Wisconsin Press
114 North Murray Street
Madison, Wisconsin 53715

The University of Wisconsin Press, Ltd.
1 Gower Street, London WC1E 6HA, England

Copyright © 1978
The Board of Regents of the University of Wisconsin System
All rights reserved

Printings 1978, 1979

Printed in the United States of America

LC 77-91063
ISBN 0-299-07544-3

Contents

Preface	7
INTRODUCTION	9
To the Instructor	11
To the Student	16
Transcription	30
Generative Formalisms	32
Distinctive Features	33
References	36
UNIT I: SYSTEMS, CLASSES, FEATURES, AND RULES	37
UNIT II: PHONOLOGICAL CONDITIONING	49
UNIT III: GRAMMATICAL CONDITIONING	69
UNIT IV: STYLE AND DIALECT	113
Sources	123
Index of Languages	125

Preface

This workbook is intended to provide a set of exercises suitable for use in courses in generative phonology. Unlike previous workbooks, therefore, it goes beyond contrast and complementation to the analysis of feature systems, natural classes, redundancy, rules and rule orderings, and the effect of grammar (morphosyntax) on phonology. In addition, in view of recent generative interest in dialectology and sociolinguistics, an attempt has been made to include representative problems in stylistic and dialectal variation.

The following Introduction should be read carefully. "To the Instructor" explains how the workbook is organized and how it can be keyed to the materials covered in a generative phonology class. "To the Student" explains how, given the Focus statements preceding each exercise. the student can proceed to analyze the data and formulate a generative solution. It also provides programmed analyses of two sample problems. Afterwards, a list of phonetic symbols and generative formalisms is given for reference.

Although this workbook is primarily designed for a generative audience, it is hoped that other schools, too, might profitably use it. To this end, the Focus statements specify as simply and neutrally as possible the phenomena to be observed and accounted for. If a non-generative approach is desired, the instructor has only to substitute the methodology he/she prefers for that outlined in the following sections. The Focus statements themselves are flexible enough to permit several approaches to the data.

The exercises have been tried out in phonology courses here at West Virginia University. Special thanks are due to:
1. my students, for their help in working out the inevitable bugs;
2. my wife Mary Jo, for her patience with a husband tied to the typewriter;
3. Gary Harris, Renate Benkert, and Wellingda Sousa, for helping with some of the Russian, Polish, German, and Portuguese data;
4. the University of Wisconsin Press, for supporting a very complex project; and
5. the many authors whose works were consulted for these exercises; the debt owed them is far greater than mere listing under "Sources" can indicate.

M. Stanley Whitley
Morgantown, W. V.

Introduction

To the Instructor

"Generative phonology" is a theory of language which, like its congener transformational grammar, attained a definite, unified position in the mid-sixties. Since then, again like transformational grammar, it has evolved in several directions as linguists have sought answers to a variety of questions and proposed a variety of extensions, revisions, and innovations, ranging from minor to major. The present flowering of competing proposals is so great, in fact, that a recent conference on generative phonology distinguished the following:

>   natural generative phonology
>   natural phonology
>   revised standard theory
>   equational phonology
>   autosegmental phonology
>   upside-down phonology
>   atomic phonology

Undoubtedly, there are others which also descend from the "standard theory" expounded by Chomsky and Halle 1968 (SPE), and further proposals are surely in the offing. And, to complete the roster of phonologies, one must take into account the non-generative approaches--e.g., Jakobsonian phonology and other offspring of Prague, and (still in use, despite the severe critique of generativists such as Postal 1968) stratificational and "classical" (taxonomic) phonemics. To make matters even more complex, some phonologists are resolute independents, borrowing eclectically from here and there the concepts they find valuable and forging ahead individualistically elsewhere.

Consequently, there is presently a lack of agreement on many points of analysis and theory. Even within generative phonology, some linguists still observe a wake for the taxonomic phoneme while others (e.g., Schane 1973) have considered resurrecting it; some pursue marking conventions and linking rules while others discount such add-ons and seek new approaches to naturalness; some adhere to the SPE system of binary distinctive features while others suggest additional ones, even non-binary ones; and the debates over abstractness, naturalness, and extrinsic rule ordering continue with great vigor. In such an atmosphere of flux and controversy, it seems the pinnacle of temerity to submit a pedagogical resource naïvely entitled "Generative Phonology Workbook."

Yet despite the unsettled present and unforeseeable future of phonological theory, there is still consensus on basic issues, and several excellent texts have recently appeared to lay forth that consensus and explore tentatively the areas of controversy. There is no reason why a workbook should not attempt to do the same. And clearly one is needed. Although a handful of structuralist-inspired and thus structuralist-oriented workbooks are extant (e.g., Gleason 1955 and Robinson 1970), these cannot be expected to provide suitable practice in the areas of analysis which have been opened up by two decades of generative phonology. The pedagogical materials therefore have a gap.

This workbook seeks to fill the gap, at least to the extent possible in this lively period. The overriding consideration in its organization is adaptability to a variety of phonologies. To ensure this, the following principles have been observed.

1. In view of the plethora of competing theories and methodologies, specific instructions are kept to a minimum for the sake of flexibility. In general, they are limited to a brief statement called "Focus" indicating those phenomena whose distribution and behavior in various contexts are to be accounted for. At first sight, the Focus in most exercises may seem somewhat lean and even incomplete to

those who are accustomed to lengthy how-to-do-it directions. Yet in my experience students have little difficulty in proceeding from the Focus to observation of patterns and formulation of a solution, given exposure to principles and formalisms presented by teacher-_cum_-text. With a bare-bones Focus, the same data can be approached by means of a variety of analytical frameworks, with the student positing autonomous phonemes, morphophonemes, systematic phonemes, or underlying feature matrices as directed by the teacher. In fact, the same exercises can be approached very profitably in two or more ways in order to demonstrate contrasts in theory and method.

Nevertheless, it is expected that most classes using this workbook will have a generative orientation, and that for some students more specific directions may be needed than the Focus alone. Therefore the following section, "To the Student," describes in detail the types of phenomena which occur in each unit, suggests a number of strategies for analysis, presents two sample analyses, and lists for reference the formalisms of generative phonology as they appear in most standard theories. These materials should facilitate the students's use of Focus to arrive at a generative solution.

2. It should be borne in mind that this workbook is not intended as a self-sufficient introduction to phonology. Although the materials in this introduction may prove useful for reference and review, such aids are no substitute for a lucid textbook on phonology and a competent and patient phonology teacher.

3. With the exception of the sample analyses, no solutions are given for these exercises. Particularly in Units II, III, and IV, it is expected that different students tackling the same data will often come up with different solutions. Such a variety of solutions is to be encouraged, rather than stifled by prescribing one putatively "correct" solution, inasmuch as class comparison and discussion of alternative solutions is the key to the justification of phonological analyses, an important experience in linguistic analysis and argumentation.

4. Courses labeled "Phonology" differ somewhat in different universities (in fact, often within the same university as taught by different instructors). Furthermore, in a single class students vary greatly in their backgrounds, ranging from brief exposure to simple contrast and complementation in an introductory general linguistics course, to previous courses in phonetics and one or more schools of phonology. In order to serve an audience of such diversity, this workbook proceeds from bottom up, with the initial exercises in each unit being relatively simple.

Instructors with well-prepared students may wish to use these initial problems only for in-class examples, or to omit them altogether and proceed to more complex problems. Those whose students have weak analytical skills and little exposure to phonology might profitably assign such problems for self-help and catch-up work. In _no_ class is it anticipated that all the exercises will be suitable or even feasible, given time-factors and different goals, emphases, and sequencing of materials in different classes. The instructor should examine the exercises and select and sequence that subset which best conforms to the needs of his/her students and the plan of the particular course.

5. In order to aid the instructor in selecting and sequencing exercises, below is given a table outlining the topical and methodological emphases of each unit.

Introduction: To the Instructor 13

TOPICS	METHODOLOGY
phenomena focused on in the data	issues and principles implicit in a generative solution or in comparison of solutions

UNIT I

phonological contrasts	use of features to capture contrasts
vowel and consonant systems	feature matrices
natural classes	distinctive/redundant specifications
naturalness of segments	marking conventions
segmental and sequential redundancy	underlying constraints and redundancy rules
neutralization	formalization of rules

UNIT II

complementary distribution	use of features to capture generalizations
assimilation	formalisms for specifying conditioning factors precisely
effect of position-within-the-word	
syllabication of sonorants	determination of underlying units and justification thereof
devoicing and voicing	
insertion	rule-ordering
effects over word-boundaries	Greek-letter variables
	"elsewhere" condition

UNIT III

effects of formative boundaries	underlying representation of morphemes with varying surface realizations
fusion of adjacent segments	
"morphophonemic" alternations	phonological vs. grammatical conditioning
deletion of segments	formalization of grammatical conditioning
tone alternations	abstract solutions
vowel harmony	angled brackets (useful in some solutions)
metathesis	formalization of natural classes undergoing similar processes
comparison of similar rules in different languages	
	rule-ordering
	conspiracies, global rules

UNIT IV

stylistic variation	derivation of different lects from a single representation
dialectal variation	
	different orderings of rules
	low-level phonetic rules

Although the division between Units II and III roughly corresponds to that between structuralist phonemics and morphophonemics, no such theoretical distinction of levels is necessarily intended here. (Whether two levels of underlying representation are to be posited, as in structuralist but not generative schools, depends on the theoretical orientation and goals of the particular course.) The division into units merely reflects a heuristic one of "problems involving no grammatical (morphosyntactic) conditioning" and "problems involving grammatical conditioning," a progression of analytical development still reflected in generative

texts (such as those cited at the end of this Introduction). Moreover, both kinds
of data are treated in full-length generative phonologies (e.g., Harris 1969 and
Wurzel 1970). While work with complementary distribution is scarcely regarded as
the vanguard of generative theoretical development, the above table lists several
key methodological principles which can be demonstrated and practiced in such exercises. In fact, even the now banal example of English voiceless stops is worthy of
the attention of the generative phonology student; as shown in the section "To the
Student," a generative solution involves specification of a natural class with distinctive features, ordering of subparts of a rule, formalization of "elsewhere,"
angled brackets, and comparison and evaluation of descriptively adequate solutions
--all of which are vital items on the agenda of a course in generative phonology.

Some of the concerns of post-SPE phonology are not fully represented in this
workbook. For example:

Conspiracies and derivational constraints

While interesting additions to the theory, these concepts are quite recent (and
not yet universally accepted), and thus have not been in circulation long enough
to be confirmed in large enough samples of data for one to fomulate many non-Yawelmani
exercises on them. The isolation of such constraints requires attention to a block
of generative rules formulated for a language, and few languages have been subjected
to a sufficiently complete generative analysis. Nevertheless, there are two problems
(#50, #51) in Unit III which suggest possible conspiracies and derivational constraints.

Sentence-level suprasegmentals

Although there are exercises herein dealing with suprasegmentals, none involve
sentence-level phenomena. This, too, reflects a relative paucity of data. Chomsky
and Halle 1968 and sequel proposals have of course revealed much information on English, but I have presumed that where the subject is taken up, students are directly
exposed to the Nuclear Stress Rule, and therefore have not drawn up exercises using
English data. Outside of English, the literature contains very few full-length treatments from which to draw up practicable exercises.

Morphologization, telescoping, and inversion of rules

These are also given short shrift, although not for lack of data but because of
the synchronic orientation of this workbook. The questions of whether a "crazy"
rule has evolved from a more natural one, and whether two rules have reversed their
ordering (and why), are diachronic in orientation, and therefore require complex
"before" and "after" sets of data--and often several "in-between" sets as well. However, the solutions to some problems do have rather crazy rules and many require ordered rules, and in Unit IV there are dialects which evince different orderings of
the same rules. The instructor who wishes to introduce morphologization, telescoping,
and rule-inversion might use such exercises for speculative discussion, but diachronic
linguistics is worthy of its own course--and its own text and workbook. Its issues
are not specifically addressed in this workbook.

6. The data were drawn from as wide a range of languages as was possible, including European languages. While some may feel that the latter inclusions introduce an
unfair advantage to speakers and students of those languages, in my experience the
danger appears minimal. Most such students are in fact unaware of the deep phonological regularities of their languages, and profit greatly from exercises which

Introduction: To the Instructor

show phonological analysis to be as relevant to French, German, and Spanish as to Swahili, Arawak, and Papago.

7. Finally, there is the matter of transcription; phonologists do not share exactly the same arsenal of phonetic symbols. Not even within a given school of phonology is uniformity to be found.[1] Of course, the variability of transcription normally causes few real problems in most linguistic publications because the values of any unfamiliar or ambivalent symbols can usually be inferred from the expository context. But in a workbook, where there is no such surrounding exposition, transcription can pose problems.

It seems that the transcriptional system should (1) be internally consistent, (2) provide for all phones needed (which, in a workbook based on many languages, are quite a swarm), (3) avoid overuse of diacritics (which make for a peppery typography), and (4) transcend local and specialized traditions. With these considerations in mind, I have opted for a version of the International Phonetic Alphabet (IPA), as laid out in the reference materials following "To the Student."

Departures from standard IPA are limited to the following:

<u>alveopalatals</u>: following almost universal usage, š ž č ǰ replace ʃ ʒ tʃ dʒ. (For the corresponding nasal, which is not provided for in IPA, the typographically parallel ň will be used.)

<u>retroflexion</u>: for the same reason, ṭ ḍ ṣ ẓ ṇ ḷ replace ʈ ɖ ʂ ʐ ɳ ɭ.

<u>lower-low unrounded vowels</u>: IPA (including modifications proposed by Kurath and McDavid) provides a ɑ ɒ for front, central, and back, respectively. But the distinction is rarely to be observed in most transcriptions, where all three are rendered by a. The latter usage will be adopted in this workbook to avoid confusion; where necessary, diacritics will distinguish front, central, and back.

<u>palatal glide</u>: IPA j stands for both glide and fricative; where the difference is noteworthy, these phones will be distinguished by the use of j for the glide and ǰ for the fricative. Note that IPA y is a high front rounded tense vowel, not a glide.

---

[1] In the case of generative phonology, cf. Chomsky and Halle 1968, Schane 1973, Hyman 1975, Harris 1969, and Harms 1968. For example, in Harms 1968, y is an unrounded glide on p. 31, and a high front rounded vowel on p. 117 (a phone earlier represented by ü on p. 78; in IPA, this symbol represents a central vowel.)

To the Student

Phonological analysis is akin to analysis in any endeavor: one observes the data, seeks generalizations (patterns, regularities, laws) in the data, formulates a hypothesis about these generalizations, and tests it against the data to see if it works--i.e., if it is <u>adequate</u>.[2] In the event that two or more solutions are possible, one then compares those solutions to see which is simplest and most general, a step called <u>justification</u>. Some maintain that analysis (especially the hunt-the-pattern step) is governed by scientifically formulable procedures, while others insist that it is more of an art or skill that depends on the perceptiveness of the individual. It is true that some students find analysis easier than others; the same exercise will seem simple and even obvious to one student, whereas another may pore over the data for a long time without perceiving any systematic, regular pattern. (In such a case, it is often better to leave the data for a while and later come back with a fresh mind.)

This workbook is designed to develop your skill in phonological analysis by means of practice with many types of data. But analysis is only the first step in any approach to phonological data; the second is the formulation of the solution(s) according to the theoretical approach you are being introduced to in your phonology class. Several such approaches have appeared in modern linguistics, but the principal one at present is generative phonology. Generative phonology, which has evolved since the late fifties, stresses formalization of solutions in terms of a certain set of descriptive tools designed to show, as generally, simply, and explicitly as possible, the relevant facts of a plausible solution. Although these tools (features, symbols, abbreviatory devices) are summarized at the end of this Introduction for reference, it is understood that you are currently enrolled in a phonology course in which such machinery will be explained in more detail than is possible in a workbook. If the approach adopted in your class is non-generative, you may be asked to adopt a different format for stating your solutions.

The instructions for individual exercises are generally confined to a short statement called "Focus." The Focus indicates those phenomena (phones and forms) whose distribution and behavior in various environments you are to account for. In a generative analysis, you must determine how (and even whether) the phenomena in question are to be related by means of derivation from one or more underlying units. You may assume that segments <u>not</u> mentioned in the Focus are to be left unanalyzed (i.e., they are the "givens"), though in a full analysis of the language everything would have to be scrutinized.

Many exercises are broken down into graduated sections--(a), (b), (c), etc. Typically, section (a) presents the most straightforward and clearest cases. Subsequent sections introduce progressively more complex data which lead to a generalization, extension, or refinement of the analysis arrived at in the earlier sections. For example, section (a) might show nasals assimilating to the point of articulation of the following consonant while (b) might show cases where assimilation is blocked. In each such exercise, you should begin with (a) and then proceed as deeply into the following sections as you can, adapting your solution as you go. Such graduation is intended to build up your ability to perceive basic patterns first and subpatterns and extensions later. In real-life fieldwork, of course, informants do not supply data in quite this fashion.

---

[2]More precisely here, <u>observationally</u> <u>adequate</u>. Then, in justifying one analysis over another, one strives for <u>descriptive</u> <u>adequacy</u>, and eventually, <u>explanatory</u> <u>adequacy</u>. See Chomsky 1965 for a discussion of the different types of adequacy.

Introduction: To the Student 17

In several exercises with graduated sections, the last sections have their own Focus. These deal with related phenomena (not necessarily with the same pattern) from the same language, or suggest comparisons with other exercises to bring out cross-linguistic generalizations. In some sections, certain forms are left blank; here, you are to generate the missing forms in order to apply your analysis.

The Focus statements are brief because there are several "phonologies" currently taught in linguistics programs, each with slightly different frameworks for analysis and formulation. In order to amplify on these statements and clarify them, we will examine below a generative approach to the exercises in each unit. In a non-generative class, you should of course rely on the procedures outlined by your instructor and text; even in a generative one, however, the following discussion can serve only as a rough guide to analysis and formulation--here again, pay close attention to the theory and methodology introduced in your course.

UNIT I

This set of exercises emphasizes the development of facility in working with phonological features. In the first exercise, you choose the feature which distinguishes each segment from the other, and specify each as + or - for that feature (see the reference materials at the end of this Introduction for a list of distinctive features). In some cases, there is more than one difference involved in the contrast; e.g., /e/ contrasts with /o/ in rounding and backness. When you are asked (as in Exercise #2) to state which difference is distinctive and which is redundant, you must carefully consider the particular system in which the two occur; e.g., in a language whose only vowels are /i e a o u/, backness is distinctive (the main difference) while rounding is <u>redundant</u> (i.e., predictable--non-low back vowels are automatically [+round] here). In a system such as /i e a o u ɤ ɯ/, however, rounding is likewise distinctive; here, not all non-low back vowels are necessarily rounded, and in fact [±round] is needed to distinguish /o/ from /ɤ/ and /u/ from /ɯ/.

The redundancy of a feature in a matrix of feature specifications characterizing a segment is called <u>segmental redundancy</u>, and can be formalized using much the same conventions as for phonological rules. Thus, if, as in the first case mentioned above (/i e a o u/), non-low back vowels are always rounded, we can write the constraint up as in (1) below; in some generative approaches, references to rounding would then be extracted from the matrices of these vowels, simplifying them.

$$(1) \begin{bmatrix} V \\ -\text{low} \\ +\text{back} \end{bmatrix} \longrightarrow [+\text{round}] \qquad (2) \begin{bmatrix} V \\ -\text{low} \\ +\text{back} \end{bmatrix}$$
$$\downarrow$$
$$[+\text{round}]$$

(Some prefer the format shown in (2) so as to distinguish redundancy rules from other kinds of rules; either way, the arrow translates as 'implies the presence of.')

Another kind of redundancy is <u>sequential redundancy</u>. Here, a feature specification which is otherwise distinctive is predictable in certain contexts (i.e., given the surrounding sequences of other segments). For example, English /f s š θ/ generally contrast (cf. <u>fin</u>, <u>sin</u>, <u>shin</u>, <u>thin</u>), but in a word-initial cluster with a following obstruent, only /s/ can occur: <u>stick</u>, but not *<u>ftick</u>, *<u>shtick</u>, *<u>thtick</u>. In fact, we can generalize further: of all the fricatives that English has (the above plus /v ð z ž/), only /s/ is possible here—contrasts among fricatives are <u>neutralized</u> in this position. This is both a constraint on sequences of phonemes and an observation about the structure of English morphemes (i.e., a <u>morpheme structure constraint</u>); a morpheme beginning with /vg/, /ðb/, /θt/, /fp/, /žk/, etc., would be conspicuously "un-English." It can be stated as in (3).

(3) $\begin{bmatrix} +\text{consonantal} \\ +\text{continuant} \\ -\text{sonorant} \end{bmatrix} \longrightarrow \begin{bmatrix} -\text{voice} \\ +\text{coronal} \\ +\text{anterior} \\ +\text{strident} \\ -\text{high} \end{bmatrix} \quad / \: \# \_\_\_\_\_ [-\text{sonorant}]$

(We could just as well have used the type of format illustrated earlier in (2).)

After you have familiarized yourself with features and redundancy rules in Exercises #3 and 4, you might begin the search for redundancy from scratch in the data in Exercises #5-10.

In Exercise 11 you are to practice drawing up phonological rules using formalisms such as those listed at the end of this Introduction. For example, given that "nasals become syllabic word-finally after a consonant," you write:

(4) $\begin{bmatrix} +\text{consonantal} \\ +\text{nasal} \end{bmatrix} \longrightarrow [+\text{syllabic}] \: / \: C\_\_\_\_\#$

On the left of the arrow is specified just the segment (or class of segments, in this case) undergoing the change; on the right of the arrow is shown the result (the change); and all the environmental factors (neighboring segments and boundaries) which induce or condition the change but are themselves unaffected are described in the environment of the rule (that part to the right of the diagonal).

When two or more segments are affected simultaneously, a different format is called for. For example, metathesis (when two segments reverse position) and fusion (when two segments become one) require statements such as the following. ((5) metathesizes the consonants of English <u>ask</u> to produce the non-standard <u>aks</u>, and is limited to that one word; (6) fuses underlying /ər/ of English into [ɚ].

(5) # æ s k # ⟶ 1 3 2   ('given that the second segment is /s/
    1 2 3   and the third /k/, the second and third
                                             reverse.')

(6) ə r ⟶ ɚ ∅   ('given that the first of two segments
    1 2   1 2   is /ə/ and the second /r/, the first
                                       takes on the retroflexion of the second,
                                       which drops.')

Exercises #12 and 13 involve <u>natural classes</u> and <u>marking conventions</u>. For determining natural classes, you should examine the system given, state the features (if any) shared by the circled segments, and determine whether one or more of these features uniquely characterize these circled segments, but <u>none of the uncircled ones</u>, and define them as a naturally related group. For example, in the system

/(i e) a o u ʌ/

the circled segments share the specification [-back], a feature specification which is lacking in /a o u ʌ/ (which, of course, are [+back]), and therefore demarcating

Introduction: To the Student

/i e/ as a natural class.

Marking conventions are not covered in all classes, especially at the beginning, as they are rather complex and not firmly established. They have been developed in order to describe why one of two similar segments may be far more common (more "natural") than the other. For example, of the two unrounded high vowels /i/ and /ɯ/, /i/ is much more widespread (/ɯ/ striking the speakers of many languages as quite exotic and perhaps even unaesthetic); hence, if a language has only one vowel which is [-round, +high], it is more natural to expect it to be [-back] than [+back]. Put more technically, [-back] is <u>unmarked</u> ([u back]) here while [+back] is <u>marked</u> ([m back]). Put more technically:

(7) [u back] → [-back] / $\begin{bmatrix} +\text{syllabic} \\ -\text{round} \\ +\text{high} \end{bmatrix}$

Like redundancy rules, marking conventions such as (7) enable us to factor out feature specifications from underlying matrices; /i/'s value for [back] is unmarked, which makes for a simpler and more natural matrix of features for it than that of /ɯ/. This is <u>not</u> to deny the possibility of the system /ɯ e a o u/, with no /i/, in some language, but to state only that such a system would be rather weird in view of our present knowledge of typical vowel systems. Some scholars would even argue that the analysis /ɯ e a o u/ is itself weird, and might use the markedness of /ɯ/ to suggest that /i/ underlies it.

UNIT II

The Focus in each of the exercises in Unit II indicates a set of phones which may not contrast. Given (1) phonetic similarity of these phones and (2) complementary distribution, all phonologists of any banner would agree that they are realizations (<u>allophones</u>, to use the traditional term) of a single underlying unit (<u>phoneme</u>). In some schools, phonetic similarity and complementary distribution are necessary and sufficient criteria; in most generative schools, morphological alternations--encountered in Unit III--are also crucial in determining underlying representations. In this generative phonology workbook, Unit II is set off from Unit III merely to give you graduated practice with both considerations.

<u>Complementary distribution</u> refers to a situation in which one phone occurs in one set of environments while others occur in different environments, never rendezvousing to contrast in the same position. The stock example from English is the fact that unaspirated stops [p t č k] tend to be limited to positions after [s] and before word-boundary (<u>spit</u>) while aspirated stops [pʰ tʰ čʰ kʰ] tend to occur elsewhere.[3] Given the complementary distributions of [p] and [pʰ], [t] and [tʰ], etc., all phonologists would posit one underlying source, or phoneme, for each pair. In a generative analysis, we can formulate a general rule which accounts for all four phonemes as a natural class undergoing one process, as in (8) (next page). Note that the natural class is labeled simply with three features; these three suffice to characterize /p t č k/ and disqualify all other segments.

---

[3] The actual rule is somewhat more complex. Intervocalic /p č k/ vary in their aspiration, especially after a stressed vowel (<u>happy</u>, <u>touchy</u>, <u>lucky</u>). Intervocalic /t/ after a stressed vowel (<u>atom</u>) or stressed vowel + /r/ (<u>party</u>) not only is unaspirated, but merges with /d/ as a voiced flap (thus, <u>latter</u> = <u>ladder</u> in American English). Also, all four are unaspirated before stops, nasals, and fricatives (<u>duct</u>, <u>apt</u>, <u>acne</u>, <u>Atkins</u>, <u>action</u>, <u>rupture</u>). The rule discussed in this section is thus meant to be illustrative and not exhaustive.

$$(8) \quad \begin{bmatrix} \text{+consonantal} \\ \text{-continuant} \\ \text{-voice} \end{bmatrix} \longrightarrow \begin{Bmatrix} [\text{-aspirated}] \; / \; \begin{Bmatrix} \underline{}\# \\ s\underline{} \end{Bmatrix} \\ [\text{+aspirated}] \quad \text{elsewhere} \end{Bmatrix}$$

In many idiolects, however, the phone representing /t/ before nasals (as in <u>chutney</u>, <u>catnip</u>, <u>atmosphere</u>, and--with syllabic [n̩]--<u>button</u>, <u>mitten</u>, <u>satin</u>) is not [tʰ], as presently generated by (8), but glottal stop [ʔ]. In such dialects, the rule would have to be modified somehow to state that--just in case the [-voice, -continuant] consonant is a /t/ with a following nasal in the environment--a glottal stop is the output (or allophone). Such an "if..., then..." contingency could be shown as a separate rule ordered before the aspiration rule:

(9)   t ⟶ ʔ / ____[+nasal]

(10)   (= (8); rule (9) has now eliminated, or "bled," /t/ before nasals)

But the abbreviatory device known as angled brackets (⟨ ⟩) enables us to build (9) right into (10), collapsing the two rules as shown in (11).

$$(11) \quad \begin{bmatrix} \text{+consonantal} \\ \text{-continuant} \\ \text{-voice} \\ \langle \text{+coronal} \\ \text{+anterior} \rangle \end{bmatrix} \longrightarrow \begin{Bmatrix} \langle \text{ʔ} \; / \; \underline{}[\text{+nasal}] \rangle \\ [\text{-aspirated}] \; / \; \begin{Bmatrix} \underline{}\# \\ s\underline{} \end{Bmatrix} \\ [\text{+aspirated}] \quad \text{elsewhere} \end{Bmatrix}$$

Angled brackets are not the easiest formalism to digest, and might be regarded as an acquired taste. You will not often need to use them; even in the above case, (9) and (10) provide an alternative to (11). Nevertheless, in general whenever one solution collapses into one plausible rule what another expresses as two or more rules, and both solutions are adequate, then the one-rule solution is viewed as simpler, and therefore better justified.[4]

Finally, a word is due about the word "elsewhere" appearing in the above rules. Technically, this is not a standard environment in generative notation, although it might be used informally and provisionally, as in (8) and its successors. In a more formal version of (8), the "elsewhere" condition could be handled by ordering it first, as follows:

$$(8') \quad \ldots \longrightarrow \begin{Bmatrix} [\text{+aspirated}] \\ [\text{-aspirated}] \; / \; \begin{Bmatrix} \underline{}\# \\ s\underline{} \end{Bmatrix} \end{Bmatrix}$$

As reformulated, the rule will now aspirate all /p t č k/, then deaspirate them just in the specified environments. Such is the format used, for example, in Anderson and Jones 1977:25.

---

[4]Such, at least, was the case in early generative theory. At present, there is some concern about formulations that collapse into speciously simpler master-rules what may in fact be distinct, unrelated processes; i.e., simplicity may not always beget naturalness and plausibility.

Introduction: To the Student

Another format for capturing formally the notion of "elsewhere" utilizes what is called a <u>minus-rule feature</u>. Here, the "elsewhere" subcase comes last, and the contextually specified subcase stipulates [-next rule]:

$$(8'') \quad \ldots \longrightarrow \left\{ \begin{matrix} \begin{bmatrix} \text{-aspirated} \\ \text{-next rule} \end{bmatrix} & / & \left\{ \begin{matrix} \underline{\quad}^{\#} \\ s\underline{\quad} \end{matrix} \right\} \\ [\text{+aspirated}] & & \end{matrix} \right\}$$

The feature [-next rule] which is added to /p t č k/ when unaspirated prevents them from being aspirated in the second (elsewhere) subcase of the rule. Such is the format which is used in Harms 1968:73.

The minus-rule feature can also be used to express "except when..." contexts. Suppose, for example, that in a given language /s/ is voiced except when it is phrase-initial (i.e., occurs after a phrase-boundary, ‖). This can be formulated as follows.

$$(12) \quad s \longrightarrow \left\{ \begin{matrix} [\text{-next rule}] \ / \ \| \underline{\quad} \\ [\text{+voice}] \end{matrix} \right\}$$

However the elsewhere condition is treated formally, one cannot simply delete the word "elsewhere." If it were deleted in (8) without revising this rule in one of the suggested ways, then all /p t č k/ would end up aspirated. This is because rules abbreviated in curly braces are conjunctively ordered, i.e., can both apply. The format in (8') counters this by ordering the two rules in such a way that, if both must apply, then the deaspiration rule will win out in the specified environments. The format in (8") blocks conjunctive ordering explicitly with its [-next rule] feature.

In some exercises in Unit II you will observe that the surrounding phonetic environment sufficiently characterizes the different distributions of allophones of one phoneme; typically, there may be assimilation of one phoneme to a neighbor, or a segment may become syllabic or otherwise transformed because of its word position. In other cases, you may note that the same phonological rule which applies within the word also applies across word boundaries in later sections of an exercise; in formalizing such a rule, you must allow for an optionally interloping word-boundary (#). In a few exercises you will encounter <u>free variation</u>, where two phones are not in complementary distribution, but neither do they contrast. Such is the case in many American English dialects of diphthongized and nondiphthongized tense vowels-- e.g., [ej] and [e] vary freely as realizations of /e/. In other exercises, a phone is inserted predictably, and therefore non-distinctively; here the format is

$$(13) \quad \emptyset \longrightarrow X \ / \ \ldots$$

i.e., "where there was nothing before, there appears the phone <u>X</u>."

It is impossible to anticipate here all the phenomena which you will encounter in these exercises. But in order to give you a sample format for approaching the data in Unit II and formulating solutions, below is given a programmed study of one exercise. Again, there may be a few variances between this approach and that used in your class; this sample is merely illustrative of a generative approach. After scanning the data, use the questions on the left to guide you in your analysis, and check your answers and observations against those on the right.

SAMPLE 1: BRAZILIAN PORTUGUESE (CARIOCAN)
Focus: [t], [č]; [d], [ǰ].

'altitude'	alčitúǰi	'ticket'	biʎéči	'help'	ažudár
'open'	abértu	'tomato'	tomáči	'money'	ǰiɲéjru
'cellar'	adéga	'duck'	pátu	'under'	ǰibájšu
'towel'	toáʎa	'age'	idáǰi	'departure'	parčida
'ink'	číta	'twelve'	dózi	'finger'	dédu
'fast'	xápidu	'four'	kwátru	'shy'	čímidu
'port'	pórtu	'late'	tárǰi	'long'	kõprídu
'rock'	pédra	'tiger'	čígri	'death'	mórči
'building'	eǰifísjo	'lens'	léči	'potato'	batáta
'pin'	alfinéči	'stiff'	tézu	'contest'	kõpečisḗw̃

1. By "Focus" are meant those segments whose behavior is to be accounted for. First consider [t] and [č]. These two phones are quite similar; what phonological features do they have in common?

All except [high] and [delayed release] (which are − for [t] and + for [č]), and [anterior] (which is + and −, respectively).

2. Look at their distribution. Does position-within-the-word differentiate the two phones?

No; both occur initially and medially.

3. Consider, then, the segments which precede [t] and those which precede [č]. Are they different?

No; [a] and [r] can precede both, so this hypothesis is a dead-end.

4. Now consider the segments which follow [t] and [č]. Which vowel always follows [č]?

[i]

5. Does [t] ever occur in that position?

No; it precedes only other vowels and consonants.

6. Therefore, all else being equal, [t] and [č] can be considered as variant realizations (allophones) of the same underlying unit (phoneme). What are the voiced equivalents of these two allophones?

[d] and [ǰ]

7. Often, sounds in a natural class behave similarly. If so, what might we expect of [t] and [č]'s relatives, [d] and [ǰ]?

That they, too, may be allophones of one phoneme.

Introduction: To the Student   23

8. If so, then what vowel should [ǰ] precede?

[i]

9. Scan the data to verify this hypothesis. Is it borne out?

Yes.

10. State informally (in more or less plain English) the general rule for the two phonemes which underlie [t č d ǰ].

Each phoneme is represented by an alveo-palatal affricate before [i], and by an alveolar stop elsewhere.

11. Since [t] and [d] seem to be the more common representatives of the two phonemes, let us symbolize the phonemes as /t/ and /d/. However, would it be necessary to specify them as stops or affricates in their matrices?

No; such information, now predictable by phonological rule, can be omitted. It is enough to know that they are the [+coronal, -continuant, -sonorant] phonemes.

12. State formally (i.e., formalize) the phonological rule which is involved in these data; if possible, use feature notation.

WITHOUT FEATURES

$$\begin{bmatrix} t \\ d \end{bmatrix} \rightarrow \left\{ \begin{matrix} \begin{bmatrix} č \\ ǰ \end{bmatrix} / \underline{\quad} i \\ \begin{bmatrix} t \\ d \end{bmatrix} \quad \text{elsewhere} \end{matrix} \right\}$$

WITH FEATURES[5]

$$\begin{bmatrix} +cons \\ +cor \\ -sonor \end{bmatrix} \rightarrow \left\{ \begin{matrix} \begin{bmatrix} -ant \\ +del\ rel \\ +high \end{bmatrix} / \underline{\quad} \begin{bmatrix} V \\ +high \\ -back \end{bmatrix} \\ \begin{bmatrix} +ant \\ -del\ rel \\ -high \end{bmatrix} \quad \text{elsewhere} \end{matrix} \right\}$$

13. Look closely at the solution with feature notation; what advantages does it have over the one without feature notation? (Note: to students without experience with features, it may appear initially more complex; but there are two advantages here.)

(1) Feature notation explains both /t/ and /d/ undergoing this rule by virtue of their similar feature composition; i.e., it relates the two as a natural class.
(2) The "palatalization" of /t d/ is explained as assimilation to the [+high] feature specification of [i].

---

[5]This rule is tentatively given in terms of "elsewhere," which, as noted earlier, is not a formal expression. It can be eliminated in either of the two ways suggested, viz.:

$$\left\{ \begin{matrix} [\ldots] \\ [\ldots] / \underline{\quad} \begin{bmatrix} V \\ +high \\ -back \end{bmatrix} \end{matrix} \right\} \quad \text{OR} \quad \left\{ \begin{matrix} \begin{bmatrix} \ldots \\ -\text{next rule} \end{bmatrix} / \underline{\quad} \begin{bmatrix} V \\ +high \\ -back \end{bmatrix} \\ [\ldots] \end{matrix} \right\}$$

or, in this case, by specifying /t d/ as underlyingly [+ant, -del rel, -high], and reducing the rule to its affrication subcase.

UNIT III

Unit III contains a variety of problems involving both the phonological conditioning emphasized in Unit II and what can be called grammatical conditioning. In grammatical conditioning, factors such as the internal structure of the word (morpheme boundaries) and morphosyntactic characteristics (properties such as inflectional class, person, number, case, tense, syntactic category) enter into the cues which trigger a rule. The simplest type of problem in Unit III requires only that you take note of relevant formative boundaries within the word when writing up the solution. In more advanced problems, you must observe the alternating shapes (changes in consonants, vowels, suprasegmentals) of stems or affixes in various forms and account for these alternations as generally and as simply as possible.

In this latter type, you can proceed in two steps.

1. Posit the appropriate underlying units (phonemes) that will characterize each type of alternation and make it predictable from the underlying representation of the word. If possible, the underlying representation should be one of the surface alternants, though in some cases you might posit a representation with an abstract unit (i.e., one which never appears phonetically as it is phonemically). Alternatively, you might opt for a representation which alternates by virtue of a special morphological property or a rule-feature (diacritic) assigned to it.

Let's take a hypothetical example. Assume that two verbs exhibit the following forms in three tenses.

	present	past	future
'fall'	bedu	bodet	bodi
'see'	bedu	bedet	bedi

We need two distinct underlying units to differentiate the two cases, e.g., /o/ in 'fall' and /e/ in 'see' (if both had /e/, there would be no way to differentiate them). Now, we can say that /o/ becomes [e] under certain conditions (yet to be determined) while /e/ stays [e]. This solution works well, as long as these are the only data to be accounted for.

But, just to complicate matters, suppose that there is a third word which retains [o] in all its forms. (We will assume that there is no phonological cue for this [o] as opposed to the [o] ~ [e] of 'fall', as indicated here by the simplistic use of b..d in the stems of all three.)

'carry'	bodu	bodet	bodi

Now it is no longer possible to posit /o/ for the first alternation since the new example shows /o/ clearly more likely to stay variant. Here, you can go any one of three paths:

(a) set up, say, an underlying /ø/, i.e., a segment based on the frontness of [e] and the rounding of [o]. This /ø/ would never show up as [ø], but always as either [e] or [o], and is thus abstract. However, incorporated into the underlying representation of 'fall', it enables us to predict nicely whether a vowel will alternate (/ø/ → [e], [o]) or stay as it is (/e/, /o/). Thus, the three verb stems will be /bød-/, /bed-/, /bod-/.

(b) recognize an underlying /o/ in both 'fall' and 'carry' but add a special phonological trigger to the former to induce a fronting and unrounding of its /o/ to [e]. For example, you might represent the stem of 'fall' as /bodj-/ and that of 'carry' simply as /bod-/. This type of solution is likewise abstract because it sets up a unit (/j/) which appears in no surface allomorphs, but it distinguishes

Introduction: To the Student

the form which can undergo fronting and unrounding from the one which cannot. It also suggests that the reason for this change is assimilation to underlying /j/.

(c) hypothesize that--as in (b)--'fall' and 'carry' both have /o/, but that 'fall' is tagged with a rule-feature [+fronting and unrounding] (or [+FAU], for short). (Such a rule-feature would be exactly parallel to the feature [+final consonant voicing] on English words such as wife/wives, path/paths, where /f/→ [v] and /θ/→ [ð]; cf., on the other hand, cliff(s), myth(s), which, like 'carry' in this problem, do not alternate). This solution, like the other two, "works"; unlike them, it does not set up abstract units.

Deciding which path to take in accounting for alternations--(a), (b), (c)-- is an important step in evaluating and justifying solutions. Currently there is some debate on which is more justified when two or three of them yield adequate solutions, and this debate may be reflected in your class discussion.

2. After settling on the appropriate underlying units, the next task is to determine and formalize the environmental factors which induce the rules governing the alternations. If you appeal to phonological conditioning in the above hypothetical problem, then the rule which yields [e] from underlying /ø/ or /o/ (depending on the solution) must show that this occurs when [u] follows in the next syllable (as in (14)), or, perhaps more precisely, when an ending beginning with [u] follows (as in (15)). Solution (b) must furthermore allow for an intervening /j/ (as in (16)), which then drops; and solution (c) must specify [+FAU] on any /o/ which changes (as in (17)).

(14) .../____Cu

(15) .../____C+u

(16) .../____Cj+u

(17) .../____C+u
     [+FAU]

Yet you could also appeal to grammatical conditioning by expressing the environments in terms of the feature [+present]. On the basis of such limited data, it is unclear which type of conditioning makes for a more adequate solution. However, even with fuller data the choice of conditioning may prove as debatable as the choice of underlying representations. At present, many (but not all) generative phonologists tend to prefer phonological conditioning unless grammatical conditioning yields a demonstrably simpler and more general rule.

The hypothetical example illustrates a case in which a phonological rule will convert an underlying unit into one phone in one environment, another in a different environment; i.e., it changes or fills in features on the underlying unit. Other possibilities are that the phonological rule will insert a segment or delete one in order to generate all variants; or that several rules may be involved, carefully ordered to generate the correct output. Not all possibilities can be exemplified here, but a sample analysis is given on the following pages. You should again bear in mind the particular theoretical approach used in your class; the following analysis is a generative one.

SAMPLE 2: SPANISH (CASTILIAN)
Focus: stem alternations. Key to forms:

```
            1 = 1. sg. present indicative      6 = 1. sg. present subjunctive
            2 = 2. sg. present indicative      7 = 2. sg. present subjunctive
            3 = 1. pl. present indicative      8 = 1. pl. present subjunctive
            4 = 1. sg. imperfect indicative    9 = 3. pl. present subjunctive
            5 = gerund                        10 = command form
```

	'touch'	'trade'	'sin'	'blind'	'bend'	'settle'	'furnish'	'begin'
1	tóko	trwéko	péko	θjéγo	dóβlo	pwéβlo	amwéβlo	empjéθo
2	tókas	trwékas	pékas	θjéγas	dóβlas	pwéβlas	amwéβlas	empjéθas
3	tokámos	trokámos	pekámos	θeγámos	doβlámos	poβlámos	amweβlámos	empeθámos
4	tokáβa	trokáβa	pekáβa	θeγáβa	doβláβa	poβláβa	amweβláβa	empeθáβa
5	tokándo	trokándo	pekándo	θeγándo	doβlándo	poβlándo	amweβlándo	empeθándo
6	tóke	trwéke	péke	θjéγe	dóβle	pwéβle	amwéβle	empjéθe
7	tókes	trwékes	pékes	θjéγes	dóβles	pwéβles	amwéβles	empjéθes
8	tokémos	trokémos	pekémos	θeγémos	doβlémos	poβlémos	amweβlémos	empeθémos
9	tóken	trwéken	péken	θjéγen	dóβlen	pwéβlen	amwéβlen	empjéθen
10	tóka	trwéka	péka	θjéγa	dóβla	pwéβla	amwéβla	empjéθa

	'try out'	'rob'	'play'	'wrinkle'	'let'	'risk'	'agree'	'tune'
1	prwéβo	r̄óβo	xwéγo	ar̄úγo	déxo	ar̄jézγo	akwérðo	akórðo
2	prwéβas	r̄óβas	xwéγas	ar̄úγas	déxas	ar̄jézγas	akwérðas	akórðas
3	proβámos	r̄oβámos	xuγámos	ar̄uγámos	dexámos	ar̄jezγámos	akorðámos	akorðámos
4	proβáβa	r̄oβáβa	xuγáβa	ar̄uγáβa	dexáβa	ar̄jezγáβa	akorðáβa	akorðáβa
5	proβándo	r̄oβándo	xuγándo	ar̄uγándo	dexándo	ar̄jezγándo	akorðándo	akorðándo
6	prwéβe	r̄óβe	xwéγe	ar̄úγe	déxe	ar̄jézγe	akwérðe	akórðe
7	prwéβes	r̄óβes	xwéγes	ar̄úγes	déxes	ar̄jézγes	akwérðes	akórðes
8	proβémos	r̄oβémos	xuγémos	ar̄uγémos	dexémos	ar̄jezγémos	akorðémos	akorðémos
9	prwéβen	r̄óβen	xwéγen	ar̄úγen	déxen	ar̄jézγen	akwérðen	akórðen
10	prwéβa	r̄óβa	xwéγa	ar̄úγa	déxa	ar̄jézγa	akwérða	akórða

Introduction: To the Student

1. The Focus here is on stem alternations. The stem is that part which is left after all affixes have been isolated. What are the affixes (here, endings) in this exercise?

-o, -as, -ámos, -áβa, -ándo, -e, -es, -émos, -én, -a.

2. The stems of nine verbs do not alternate, i.e., are invariant in form. Which are they?

'touch, sin, bend, furnish, rob, wrinkle, let, risk, tune'

3. Given that, e.g., [tok-] never varies, do the data indicate any underlying representation other than /tok/ for the stem?

no; of course, the [t], [o], or [k] may be an allophone of another phoneme because of complementary distribution, but this is not indicated in the Focus; so, just /tok/.

4. However, some stems do vary. List those segments which alternate in such stems.

[we]~[o]: 'trade, settle, try out, agree'
[je]~[e]: 'blind, begin'
[we]~[u]: 'play'

5. Provisionally, let's make the simplest possible hypothesis about stems with alternating diphthongs and monophthongs; the underlying representation is one of the alternants. Assume it is the monophthong, i.e., that [we] ~ [o] derives from /o/. We must make sure that such an /o/ can be distinguished from non-alternating /o/. Is this possible? (I.e., is there any phonological cue for why /o/ alternates in some stems but not in others?

no; as shown by 'agree' and 'tune', alternating /o/ and non-alternating /o/ can have exactly the same segments for neighbors.

6. Then perhaps [we]~[o] derives from an underlying diphthong, /we/ (and likewise, [je]~[e] from /je/). What difficulty does this solution run up against?

in 'furnish' and 'risk' the diphthongs remain diphthongs throughout.

7. Thus this simplest hypothesis, that the source of the alternations is one of the alternants, is improbable. Let's cast about for a more abstract solution, one that derives [we]~[o] from a phoneme which is neither [we] nor [o]. One approach would be to posit an /ɔ/ for this alternation.[6] What would the source of [je]~[e] be then?

/ɛ/ would be exactly parallel for a diphthong alternating with the front vowel [e].

8. What feature would be needed to distinguish alternating from non-alternating mid vowels?

[±tense]

---

[6] Although /ɔ/ may appear arbitrary, there are signs pointing to a mid lax vowel for [we]~[o]. First, the monophthongal variant ([o]) and the nucleus of the diphthong ([e]) are both mid vowels. Second, lax vowels tend to be less stable and more prone to "fracture" than tense vowels. (See footnote 8 for an English example of diphthongizing lax vowels.)

9. With this approach, we can now state quite simply that [-tense] mid vowels diphthongize in certain environments while [+tense] mid vowels do not. Formalize the rule for diphthongization, ignoring for the moment the environment. (You will need to show precisely how the correct glides are inserted and how the nuclei of both diphthongs become [e].)

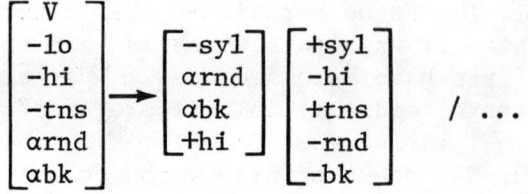

10. For the single case of [we]~[u] in [xweɣ]~[xuɣ], we could set up another lax vowel, /ʊ/ (based on the highness and backness of the [u]), and incorporate it into the above rule. However, there is an easier way to account for this single alternation after /x/. Does [we]~[o] ever follow /x/?

no

11. Hence, we can say that the same unit which underlies [we]~[o] underlies [we]~[u], namely _____. State informally how the two outputs can be distinguished.

/ɔ/; when undergoing diphthongization, this phoneme always becomes [we]; otherwise, it raises to [u] after /x/ and tenses to [o] in all other cases. (If you were able to anticipate this possibility, congratulate yourself.)

12. Many generative phonologists would argue that a solution based on /ɔ/ and /ɛ/ is excessively abstract because it posits machinery ([±tense]) that is otherwise unmotivated. In what way is [±tense] unmotivated?

It never appears in any surface contrasts, and has been instituted solely to distinguish between mid vowels that diphthongize from those which do not.

13. Instead of marking the vowel of 'agree' as [-tense] and that of 'tune' as [+tense], such phonologists would set up /o/ in both. What would be the only means of discerning 'agree' from 'tune' then?

marking one stem as [+diphthong rule] and the other [-diphthong rule]--or [±D], for short.

14. What name is given to non-phonological, non-morphosyntactic features such as "±D"?

diacritics, or rule features

15. If this solution is adopted for stems with [we]~[o] (and [we]~[u]), how would [je]~[e] stems be handled?

likewise with /e/ in the stem, and the feature [+D] on the stem.

16. Whichever underlying representation you decide on, you must still account for the environment of the diphthongization rule. Again, scan the data. There are two possibilities--the rule is sensitive to grammatical conditioning, or to phonological conditioning. What would the environment be in the first case?

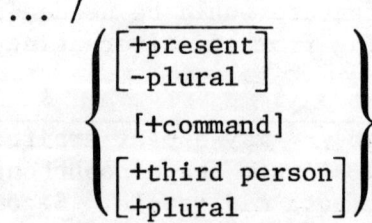

17. This is a rather complex environment, though not excluded a priori <u>unless</u> phonological conditioning yields a tidier and more natural environment. Look closely at all the diphthongized

Introduction: To the Student

forms of verb stems which alternate. What phonological feature is always present?

[+stress]

18. In these alternations, are the monophthongs [o], [e], [u] ever stressed?

no

19. How is this solution for the environment superior to the earlier one?

It reduces the conditioning factors to just one natural one, and is thus simpler.

20. Formalize now the complete rule for all alternations in the data.

ABSTRACT SOLUTION

$$\begin{bmatrix} V \\ -lo \\ -hi \\ -tns \\ \alpha rnd \\ \alpha bk \end{bmatrix} \rightarrow \begin{bmatrix} -syl \\ \alpha rnd \\ \alpha bk \\ +hi \end{bmatrix} \begin{bmatrix} +syl \\ -hi \\ +tns \\ -rnd \\ -bk \end{bmatrix} / \underline{\quad} [+stress]$$

DIACRITIC SOLUTION

$$\begin{bmatrix} V \\ -lo \\ -hi \\ \alpha rnd \\ \alpha bk \\ +D \end{bmatrix} \rightarrow \begin{bmatrix} -syl \\ \alpha rnd \\ \alpha bk \\ +hi \end{bmatrix} \begin{bmatrix} +syl \\ -hi \\ +tns \\ -rnd \\ -bk \end{bmatrix} / \underline{\quad} [+stress]$$

21. Is it understood in this formulation that, in the environment of [-stress], (=elsewhere), the underlying units will stay the same?

yes; thus the first solution requires a subsequent rule for converting [-tense] to [+tense], and both need a further rule for raising the stem-vowel of 'play' after /x/.

UNIT IV

Unit IV contains problems on stylistic and geographical variation. In some theories of sociolinguistics and dialectology it has been suggested that different styles and dialects of the same language can be described and related by positing a single underlying phoneme from which the variants are derived by phonological rule. Given that lect A has [a] where lect B has [æ], we could say that the language embracing both has a single phoneme for both, with [a] and [æ] being derived by phonological rule from that phoneme. The possibilities here are the same as for Unit III—the underlying unit may be one of the variants or distinct from (more abstract than) any of them. Rule-ordering is also important, and in some cases where several dialects are compared, different orderings of the same rules describe succinctly the phonetic differences between those dialects. Furthermore, as phonetic detail is important in some problems, you may have to introduce n-ary features (features with values of 1, 2, 3, etc. instead of the binary + or -). There is currently some debate over whether surface-phonetic contrasts can be described with simple binary features.

Transcription

	bilabial	labiodental	interdental	dental, alveolar	alveo-palatal	palatal	velar	uvular	pharyngeal	glottal
STOP voiceless	p			t		c	k	q		ʔ
voiced	b			d		ɟ	g	ɢ		
voiced implosive	ɓ			ɗ		ʄ	ɠ			
FRICATIVE voiceless	ɸ	f	θ	s	š	ç	x	χ	ħ	h
voiced	β	v	ð	z	ž	ʝ	γ	ʁ	ʕ	ɦ
NASAL (voiced)	m	ɱ		n	ň	ɲ	ŋ	ɴ		
LATERAL voiced sonorant				l		ʎ				
voiceless fricative				ɬ						
voiced fricative				ɮ						

R-SOUNDS
Unless finer distinctions are called for, the symbol <u>r</u> is customarily used for the following phones:

ɾ = alveolar flap   ɹ = alveolar approximant   ř = alveolar trill with
                                                              friction (stridency)
r̄ = alveolar trill   ʀ = uvular trill

GLIDES

j = front unrounded (palatal)   ɥ = front rounded

w = back rounded (labiovelar)   ɯ = back unrounded

OTHER CONSONANT SYMBOLS AND DIACRITICS

č = tš̬   X' = glottalized, ejective   X̣ = retroflex

ǰ = dž̬   Xʰ = aspirated   X̥ = voiceless

ʇ = alveolar click   Xʷ = rounded, labialized   X̩ = syllabic

ʗ = alveopalatal click   Xʲ = palatalized   X̪ = dental

ʖ = lateral click   X: = long   X̃ = velarized, 'emphatic'

ç⎫ (see discussion following   X̄ = tense, fortis   ⁿX = prenasalized
z̧⎭   "Distinctive Features")

Transcription

VOWELS

	UNROUNDED				ROUNDED		
	front	central	back		front	central	back
HIGH	i	ɨ	ɯ		y	ʉ	u
	ɪ				ʏ		ʊ
MID	e	ɜ	ɤ		ø	ɵ	o
	ɛ	ə	ʌ		œ		ɔ
LOW	æ	ɐ					ɒ
		a					

Note: the single symbol <u>a</u> is used for any unrounded "lower-low" vowel, whether back central, or front (IPA [a], [ɑ], [ɒ], respectively) unless finer distinctions are needed. Unless otherwise indicated, <u>a</u> can be assumed to be [+back], its unmarked value.

VOWEL DIACRITICS AND OTHER SYMBOLS

ɜ˞ ɚ } = coronalized central vowels with constriction (retroflexion, "<u>r</u>-coloring")

V˃ = backed

V˂ = fronted

V̈ = centralized

Ṽ = nasalized

Vː = long

V̥ = voiceless

V̯ = nonsyllabic

V́ = stress; high pitch

V̀ = secondary stress; low pitch

V̂ = falling pitch

V̌ = rising pitch

ABBREVIATIONS

In order to economize on space, morphosyntactic labels are frequently abbreviated. Except for the following common abbreviations, they will always be explained in the Focus of the problem.

   m. = masculine sg. = singular 1. = first person

   f. = feminine   pl. = plural   2. = second person

                    3. = third person

Generative Formalisms

A → B /...	"A goes to, is rewritten as, B in the environment of..."
___A	"before A"
B___	"after B"
___#	"before word-boundary (i.e., word-finally)"
#___	"after word-boundary (i.e., word-initially)"
+___	"after a formative (morpheme) boundary." But the symbol "=" is used for prefix boundary if prefix and suffix boundaries have different phonological effects.
___(A)B	"before B, even if A intervenes." This collapses the environments of two rules, /__AB and /__B, into one. If crucial, it is understood that the expansion AB is disjunctively ordered before the expansion B; i.e., B applies only if AB does not.
{___A / B___}	"before A or after B." Two rules thus combined are understood to be conjunctively ordered; i.e., both may apply if their conditions are met, as would be the case here with the environment B__A
___ ‖	"before a pause"; used by extension for a phrase-boundary.
C_1^3	C = any consonant; V = any vowel. When these symbols bear superscript and/or subscript numbers, the numbers indicate the upper and lower range of the number of consonants and vowels in a row. Thus C_1^3 means "from one to three consonants."
C_0^2___	"after C, CC, or no consonants at all"
___C_0	"before any number of consonants, including none at all." Given a lower limit but no upper limit, the latter is understood as "∞".
/___ [+back]	"when specified with the feature [+back]"
A → [αback] / ___ B [αback]	"A takes on the same value of the feature [back] as the following segment B." "α" is a variable ranging over "+" and "-"; when A and B are both "α" for a feature, then if B has +, A has +; if B has -, A has -. Variables thus express assimilation; dissimilation can be shown with "α" on one segment and "-α" on the other. If further variables are needed, proceed deeper into the Greek alphabet: α β γ δ ε ζ η etc.
A → [+back, <-low>] / ___⟨C⟩V́	"A takes on the feature specification [+back] when before a stressed vowel and, additionally--just in case a consonant intervenes--it becomes [-low] as well." Angled brackets,⟨ ⟩, enclose the parts of an "if..., then..." subrule; rules thus combined are understood to be disjunctively ordered.

Distinctive Features

A number of distinctive-feature systems are now extant. One of the earliest binary systems ('binary' = either + or - for a feature) was that devised by R. Jakobson, still in use in some schools. The system which is now standard in generative phonology was developed later by Chomsky and Halle and is given below. For more on feature systems, see Chomsky and Halle 1968, Schane 1973, Hyman 1975, Ladefoged 1971, Harms 1968, or any of the increasing number of articles on the subject.

These features can be abbreviated as suggested by the underlined letters.

[+syllabic]: serving as syllable peak (vowels, syllabic nasals and liquids)

[+sonorant]: characterized by full resonance (vowels, nasals, liquids, glides); some prefer to use the reverse feature, [+obstruent] (= [-sonor]).

[+consonantal]: constriction involving contact or near-contact at a point of articulation (obstruents, nasals, liquids).

[+continuant]: oral cavity not blocked off completely (vowels, glides, liquids, fricatives); chiefly used for distinguishing fricatives from stops.

[+delayed release]: stop articulation released slowly with friction (affricates).

[+strident]: relatively higher-pitched noise or turbulence in certain fricatives and affricates ([f s š χ]; [ɸ θ ç x] = [-strid]).

[+nasal]: velum lowered, resulting in nasal resonance (nasals, nasalized vowels).

[+lateral]: laterals; principal use is for distinguishing these from r-sounds.

[+anterior]: articulated in front of the alveopalatal area (labials, dentals, alveolars); more or less equatable with R. Jakobson's [diffuse].

[+coronal]: blade or apex of tongue raised (dentals, alveolars, alveopalatals, retroflex); more or less equatable with R. Jakobson's [acute].

[+high]: body of tongue raised (high vowels, glides, alveopalatals, palatals, palatalized consonants, velars, labiovelars).

[+low]: body of tongue lowered (low vowels, pharyngeals).

[+back]: body of tongue retracted (back vowels and glides, velars, labiovelars, uvulars, velarized consonants).

[+voice]: vibration of vocal cords

[+round]: articulated with lip-rounding; labialized.

[+tense]: produced with a deliberate, distinct gesture involving relatively greater length and muscular effort (fortis consonants, trills, [i e y ø u o ɜ ɤ]).

[+distributed]: involving relatively broader contact between articulators; thus, in the pairs alveolar/dental, alveopalatal/retroflex, bilabial/labiodental, the first position is [+distr] and the second is [-distr].

ALSO: [+vocalic], [+long], [+aspirated], [+stress], [+click] (or [+velaric suction]), [+implosive] (or [+glottalic suction]), [+ejective] (or [+glottalic pressure]).

It occasionally happens that a justifiable distinction or relationship cannot be captured with the standard set of features given above. For example, in Problem #46, Unit III, you will work with the Polish "soft" sibilants (IPA [ɕ], [ʑ] or ś, ź as Polish orthography renders them), which contrast both with [s], [z] and with [š], [ž]. Articulatorily, the soft sibilants are formed by laminal contact with the roof of the mouth from the alveolae into the palatal area; like [s], [z], but unlike [š], [ž] and other fricatives, they are grooved. Acoustically, furthermore, they are strident; their turbulence is less noisy than that of [š], [ž], but high-pitched like that of [s], [z]. Yet, despite the clear distinctions of the three sets of Polish sibilants, the current set of features fails to differentiate them, as shown below.[7] (The palatals [ç], [ɟ] are included for comparison.)

	s z	š ž	ɕ ʑ	ç ɟ
anterior	+	-	-	-
coronal	+	+	+	-
strident	+	+	+	-
high	-	+	+	+
distributed	+	+	+	+

Barring redefinition of the relevant features, there is no clear way to capture the distinction between the soft sibilants and the normal alveopalatals other than by appeal to a new feature. Fortunately, this kind of dilemma is fairly rare, but the literature (e.g., Ladefoged 1971) documents several such cases in which a language differentiates to a greater degree than is allowed for by current features. Other areas needing further research include coarticulation, labialization, breathy voice (murmur), creaky voice (laryngealization), r-sounds, and vowel systems with more than the three heights and two backness values allotted by [high], [low], and [back]. When you encounter such cases, you may have to propose your own features.

One other caveat for the use of distinctive features will be given here: the feature specifications of a particular systematic phoneme in a particular system may depend crucially on the phonology of the language. For example, the vowel /ɛ/ has been described as [+low] in French and as [-low, -tense] in English by Hyman. Since features are universal (with the same features used for all languages), and since, after all, [±low] has natural grounding in a real articulatory gesture, some might object that an /ɛ/ must be either [+low] or [-low] regardless of the language. But no contradiction is involved here. /ɛ/ in French is regarded as low because it --like other "low" vowels--can be nasalized; furthermore, if one ignores the obsolescent distinction [aˤ], [aˀ], it is as low as any front vowel can be in the French system. In English, however, it acts like a lax vowel,[8] and--in English--is not the lowest front vowel (which is /æ/).

This discussion is not meant to confuse you, but only to point out that, unlike phonetics, phonology is ultimately described in terms of the ways in which units function and are patterned in a given language; and that is one of the things that are interesting about phonology.

---

[7] These feature specifications are those given by Chomsky and Halle 1968, ch. 7.
[8] For example, /ɛ/ may add a schwa offglide in many American dialects: bed [bɛəd], like bid [bɪəd], bad [bæəd], bawdy [bɔədi]. See Kurath and McDavid 1961 for the geographical distribution of this offglide.

Distinctive Features

The Segmentation Problem

Drawing up feature matrices for segments presupposes that "segments" are well-defined. Acoustically and articulatorily, each segment of a word such as <u>pan</u> merges smoothly with the next, forming a sound continuum. Yet language operates as if the continuum were segmented into discrete units, phonemes on the systematic phonemic level (/pæn/) and phones on the systematic phonetic level ([pʰæ̃n]). Segments on each level are represented by matrices of feature specifications.

Since the data in this workbook are presented in terms of preanalyzed phonetic segments, you will not often have to deal with the question of how a word is to be segmented phonetically. However, phonemically some sounds may be ambivalent; depending on how they function in a given language, they may be interpreted as <u>monophonemic</u> (a single underlying segment) or as <u>biphonemic</u> (derived from a cluster or sequence of two other phonemes).[9]

<u>sequence of two phonemes?</u>

1. stop + fricative: tš ts pf tɬ
2. stop + /h/: ph th bh
3. consonant + glide: kw pj ɣw
4. geminate: ii εε tt
5. /h/ + sonorant: hl hr hm hw
6. consonant + /ʔ/: tʔ bʔ
7. velar + labial: kp gb ŋm
8. nasal + stop: mb nd ŋg
9. vowel + sonorant: ɔn ər
   ən əl əm
10. vowel + vowel: ei ou ua
    vowel + glide: ej ow wa

<u>or a single indivisible phoneme?</u>

1. affricate: č ts pf tɬ
2. aspirated stop: pʰ tʰ bʰ
3. rounded/palatalized consonant: kʷ pʲ ɣʷ
4. long: i: ε: t:
5. voiceless sonorant: ɬ r̥ m̥ w̥
6. ejective, implosive: t' ɓ
7. labiovelar: k͡p g͡b ŋ͡m
8. prenasalized stop: ᵐb ⁿd ᵑg
9. nasalized/retroflex vowel: õ ɚ
   syllabic sonorant: n̩ ɫ̩ m̩
10. vowel (non-distinctive offglide): e o

The usual considerations which guide the choice of one interpretation over the other are <u>economy</u> (reduction of the total number of phonemes needed), <u>constant association</u> (when one of the two components is limited to the combination), overall <u>structural pattern</u> (how the proposed phoneme, or sequence of phonemes, fits into the general phonological pattern of the language), and behavior in, and effect on, <u>phonological rules</u>. Sample arguments:

1. Spanish [ɾ] vs. [r̄] could be either (1) /r/ vs. /r̄/, or (2) (with the trill being interpreted as a geminate) /r/ vs. /rr/. The latter solution economizes on the number of phonemes needed, but creates a geminate, which is contrary to the overall pattern of the language (there are no other geminates).
2. English [ɚ ɫ̩ n̩] are regarded as phonemic sequences of /ə/ + sonorant (thus /ər əl ən/) because (1) this reduces the number of syllabic phonemes in English (economy), and (2) it brings the distribution of /ə r l n/ into line with that of other phonemes.
3. Breton long consonants ([tɔmːa] 'drive') could be analyzed as geminates (thus [mː] = /mm/) because (1) this economizes on the number of consonant phonemes needed and (2) long consonants cause laxing of preceding mid vowels, just as consonant clusters do (cf. [skɔlju], [skol] 'schools, school').
4. Mandarin Chinese [pʰ tʰ cʰ kʰ] are regarded as monophonemic, not phonemic clusters (/ph th ch kh/) because there is no independent /h/ phoneme occurring separately; i.e., aspiration is constantly associated with aspirated voiceless stops.

---

[9]Terms from Martinet 1939. For more information on ambivalent articulations, see also Pike 1947:131-136 (structuralist analysis) and Campbell 1974:59-63 (a proposal for feature analysis).

References

Anderson, John M. and Charles Jones, *Phonological Structure and the History of English*, Amsterdam: North-Holland, 1977.

Campbell, Lyle, "Phonological Features: Problems and Proposals," *Language* 50: 52-65, 1974.

Chomsky, Noam, *Aspects of the Theory of Syntax*, Cambridge, Mass.: the MIT Press, 1965.

Chomsky, Noam and Morris Halle, *The Sound Pattern of English*, New York: Harper and Row, 1968.

Gleason, Harry A., *Workbook in Descriptive Linguistics*, New York: Holt, Rinehart and Winston, 1955.

Harms, Robert, *Introduction to Phonological Theory*, Englewood Cliffs, N. J.: Prentice-Hall, 1968.

Harris, James, *Spanish Phonology*, Cambridge, Mass.: The MIT Press, 1969.

Hyman, Larry, *Phonology--Theory and Analysis*, New York: Holt, Rinehart and Winston, 1975.

Jakobson, Roman and Morris Halle, *Fundamentals of Language*, The Hague: Mouton, 1965.

Kurath, Hans and Raven McDavid, *The Pronunciation of English in the Atlantic States*, Ann Arbor: University of Michigan Press, 1961.

Ladefoged, Peter, *Preliminaries to Linguistic Phonetics*, Chicago: University of Chicago Press, 1971.

Martinet, André, "Un ou deux phonèmes?", *Acta Linguistica* 1:94-103 (1939).

Pike, Kenneth L., *Phonemics*, Ann Arbor: University of Michigan Press, 1947.

Postal, Paul M., *Aspects of Phonological Theory*, New York: Harper and Row, 1968.

Robinson, Dow F., *Workbook for Phonological Analysis*, Santa Ana, Cal.: Summer Institute of Linguistics, 1970, 1974.

Schane, Sanford A., *Generative Phonology*, Englewood Cliffs, N. J.: Prentice-Hall 1973.

Wurzel, Wolfgang, *Studien zur deutschen Lautstruktur*, Studia Grammatica VIII, East Berlin, 1970.

Unit I

Systems, Classes, Features, and Rules

Unit I   39

1. MINIMAL DISTINCTIONS
   Determine the distinctive feature(s) differentiating the phones in each pair.

1. ɪ ʊ	14. j w	27. l ʎ	40. b ɓ
2. a ã	15. ɛ ɛː	28. s θ	41. p p'
3. a ʌ	16. o ɤ	29. g ɣ	42. l ɬ
4. a ɒ	17. ə ɚ	30. f ɸ	43. ɾ r̄
5. u y	18. b d	31. ç x	44. z ʐ
6. ø e	19. t k	32. k q	45. n n̥
7. ɛ ɔ	20. d ð	33. š x	46. t ṭ
8. i ɯ	21. s z	34. j̇ j	47. g ŋ
9. u ʊ	22. l r	35. h ʔ	48. x ħ
10. e i	23. n ɲ	36. t ts	49. t tː
11. æ a	24. m m̥	37. d dʲ	50. β w
12. e e̥	25. p β	38. l ɬ	51. p pʰ
13. i j	26. š č	39. ɣ ʁ	52. k kʷ

2. VOWEL AND CONSONANT SYSTEMS
   Draw up feature matrices for each system, showing which feature specifications
   are distinctive and which are redundant. (Based on Ruhlen 1976.)

ABKHAZIAN: ɨ a

ALEUT: i u a

SALISHAN: i u ə a

CAMPA: i e o a

SWAHILI: i e a o u

PERSIAN: i e æ u o ɒ

DANISH: i ɪ y ʏ u ʊ o ɔ ɛ œ æ
        iː ɪː yː ʏː uː ʊː oː ɔː ɛː iːy ɪːy ɒː

KANAKANABU: i e ɯ ɤ a u o

VIETNAMESE: i e ɛ æ u o ɔ ɯ ɤ ʌ a

MANDARIN: i e y u o a

TURKISH: i e u ø y o ɯ a

PORTUGUESE: i e ɛ a ɔ u ĩ ẽ ɐ̃ õ ũ

YUKAGHIR: i e ø æ u o iː eː øː æː uː oː

CONTINUED→

HAWAIIAN

```
p       k   ʔ
            h
m   n
    l
w
```

CHEROKEE

```
    d   g
    s   z   h
        z
m   n
    l
    w   j
```

SUENA

```
pʰ  tʰ  kʰ
b   d   g
    dz
    s͡
m   n
    ɾ
w       j
```

FANTE

```
p   t   k   kʷ
b   d   g   gʷ
    f   s       h   hʷ
m       n
        r
            j       w
```

CANTONESE

```
p   t   cç  k   kʷ
pʰ  tʰ  cçʰ kʰ  kʰʷ
    f       ç       h
    n               ŋ
    l
            j   w
```

SWEDISH

```
p   t       k
b   d       g
f   s   ç       h
v       ɟ
m   n       ŋ
    l
    r̥
```

HEBREW

```
p   t       k       ʔ
b   d       g
    ts
    s͡
f   s   š   x       h
v
m   n
    l
    j               ʀ
```

EWE

```
        č       k   k͡p
b   ɖ   d   ɟ   g   gb
ɸ   f   ts  s   x
β   v   dz  z   ɣ       ʕ
m       n͡
        l
```

BASQUE

```
p   t       c       k
b   d       ɟ       g
        ts  ts͡
    f   s   ṣ
m   n       ɲ
    l       ʎ
    ɾ
    r
    j
```

YAKUT

```
p   t   č       k
b   d   ɟ       g
    s           χ   h
                ʁ
m   n       ɲ   ŋ
    l       ʎ
    ř
        j
        ɟ
```

KIRGHIZ

```
p   t           k
b   d           g
    ts  č
        ǰ
    s   š
    z   ž
m   n           ŋ
    l
    r
w       j
```

WELSH

```
p   t           k
b   d           g
    f   θ   s   š   x   h
    v   ð
m
        n   l   ɬ
            r̥
            r°
w           j
```

MASAI

```
p   t       c       k
ɓ   ɗ       ʄ       ɠ
f   s       š
m   n       ɲ       ŋ
    l
    ɾ
w           j       ʔj
    ẇ       ɟ̇
```

Unit I 41

3. SEGMENTAL REDUNDANCY
   Formalize the following constraints.

   1. All back consonants are non-low.
   2. All vowels are non-consonantal.
   3. If a vowel is high back or mid back, then it is also round.
   4. No vowels are nasal.
   5. Language V has alveolar consonants, but no alveopalatals.
   6. All liquids are alveolar.
   7. All front vowels are unrounded.
   8. All nasals are sonorant and voiced.
   9. Language W lacks affricates, but has normal stops and fricatives.
   10. Language X has the fricatives /f s š x/, but not /ɸ θ ç χ/.
   11. Language Y has only two nasals: /m n/.
   12. Language Z has only two glottalized (ejective) consonants: /p' t'/.
   13. All glides are voiced sonorants.
   14. Dental/alveolar specifications are not relevant to the descriptions of vowels.
   15. Liquids are frictionless.

4. SEQUENTIAL REDUNDANCY AND MORPHEME STRUCTURE
   Formalize the following constraints.

   1. Glide + vowel and vowel + glide exist, but not any vowel + vowel sequences.
   2. Two obstruents forming a cluster must consist of fricative + stop.
   3. If the first member of an initial cluster is a stop or fricative, the second must be a glide or liquid.
   4. All morphemes are monosyllabic, the nucleus consisting of a vowel optionally followed by a glide, and the onset and coda consisting of one, two, or no consonants.
   5. The only fricative permitted before obstruents is a voiceless alveopalatal.
   6. All vowels within a word are either rounded or unrounded, depending on the first vowel.
   7. All penultimate vowels are stressed.
   8. The second vowel within a word is stressed.
   9. An intervocalic consonant must be voiced. (Assume a syllable structure of CVCV...)
   10. All voiceless stops are aspirated before pause.
   11. The palatal glide can follow labials and velars, but not alveolars and alveopalatals.
   12. Language X distinguishes three tones, high, mid, and low; but the first vowel within a word can have only the low tone.
   13. Tense and lax vowels contrast only before one or more consonants; word-finally, only tense vowels occur.
   14. The contrast between the nasals of Language Y is neutralized word-finally; in this position, only /ŋ/ occurs.
   15. The words of Language Z begin with at most two consonants or two obstruents + one liquid.
   16. The presence of glottal stop adjacent to consonants is distinctive, but it is not distinctive between vowels, since all V + V sequences are broken up by the insertion of [ʔ].

42   Unit I

5. TAGALOG
   Focus: first, construct a vowel system consisting of five pairs; second, notice
         that in each pair more than one feature is involved in the contrast betwen
         the two phonetically. Determine which of the features is systematically
         (phonemically) distinctive, and then write a redundancy rule for the non-
         distinctive feature(s).

   (a) (within a phrase)

   ʔʌgʌd   'immediately'   haːnɪmʊn   'honeymoon'

   buːkʌs   'tomorrow'   tuːtɔh   'house'

   gʌlɪŋ   'excellence'   kʌpɛh   'coffee'

   kiːlɔs   'action'   baːlʌŋ   'locust'

   gʌbɪh   'night'   tʌluːkʌb   'crab's shell'

   ŋiːpɪn   'teeth'   dʌmɪt   'clothing'

   bʊnsɔʔ   'youngest child'   boːlʌh   'ball'

   naːjɔn   'town'   ʔʊbɔh   'cough'

   ʔɔtɔmoːbɪl   'automobile'   beːntʌh   'sale'

   bʊkʌs   'open'   gruːpɔh   'group'

   gaːlɪŋ   'from'   suːlʌt   'letter'

   ʔaːtɛh   'elder sister'   sʌŋʌh   'branch'

   gaːbɪh   'yam'   peːrʌh   'money'

   (b) All the above words have an alternative pronunciation (exemplified below)
       when occurring before a pause (i.e., phrase-finally). Write a redundancy
       rule covering final vowels within a phrase and at the end of a phrase;
       then generate the pre-pause version of the words in (a) which do not ap-
       pear below.

   ʔʌgaːd   haːnɪmuːn

   buːkaːs   tuːtoːh

   gʌliːŋ   kʌpeːh

   kiːloːs   baːlaːŋ

Unit I

6. CHUMASH
Focus: constraint on occurrence of strident segments (here, sibilants).

(a)
osos	'heel'	ats'is	'beard'	šiš	'gopher's hole'
pšoš	'gopher snake'	šoqš	'gall'	ič'ič	'younger sibling'
jasis	'poison oak'	šošo	'flying squirrel'	č'ijuš	'break wind'

(b)
| katskaw | 'I sin' | kiškin | 'I saved it' | šišk'ij | 'it aches' |
| ačkawiš | 'a sin' | skinus | 'I saved it for him' | sisk'ijus | 'he has an ache' |

7. ARABIC
Focus: constraints on occurrence of velarized and non-velarized dentals, and relationship to distribution of [a], [æ].

(a)
fiḏ:a	'silver'	ʔaɫ:a	'God'	ɫabšuːɣa	'piece of chalk'
ʔæːb	'August'	rædːæ	'he returned her'	siɫːaʕš	'sixteen'
ʔaːḍi	'judge'	ħæmː	'heat'	sæjːæːræ	'car'
ʔæːl	'he said'	ʔusːa	'story'	ɫɫatːaʕš	'thirteen'
ʕæmː	'uncle'	luʔːa	'shake it'	maḍa	'it passed'
bæsː	'enough'	faḍɫ	'kindness'	ʔasfaɣ	'yellow'
sawɫ	'noise'	ɣabaɫ	'he tied'	ʔasaḍ	'he meant'
ɣæːli	'expensive'	ħdæʕš	'eleven'	mæski	'handle'
ɫamː	'he covered up'	ẓabaɫ	'he perfected'	buːz	'mouth'
birː	'righteousness'	læʔːiːs	'late'	buːẓ	'icy cold'
ʕæːm	'he floated'	ṣaɫaḍa	'salad'	mædæ	'extent'

(b)
| nusː | 'middle' | miːn | 'who' | tiːn | 'figs' |
| ɫiːn | 'mud' | niːsæːn | 'April' | ʔibn | 'son' |

(c) Is the distribution of velarization entirely predictable (i.e., redundant)? Why or why not?

8. CZECH
Focus: distinctiveness or nondistinctiveness of (1) stress, (2) of syllabic liquids

tr̝í	'three'	kísela:	'sour'	vl̩na	'wool'
čí:slo	'number'	úbohi:	'poor'	klóbowk	'cat'
ɦláva	'head'	rádʲitʲi	'advise'	mnóho	'much'
fšúde	'everywhere'	l̩stʲivi:	'crafty'	zábava	'party'
tlústi:	'fat'	vhót	'handy'	pšenʲitse	'wheat'
ɦínowtʲi	'perish'	sr̩ttse	'heart'	úvnʲitr̝	'inside'
mráf	'manner'	žénʲix	'bridegroom'	fíjalka	'violet'
hr̝ében	'comb'	čtvr̩t	'quarter'	bá:tʲi	'lie'
ángliji	'England'	má:slo	'butter'	kmótr̩	'godfather'

9. SPANISH
Focus: contrast between [r̄] and [r] (= [ɾ]); where is it not distinctive?

kór̄o	'I run'	káro	'dear'	árte	'art'
estráɲo	'strange'	dár	'give'	r̄wéɣo	'I beg'
preferír	'prefer'	r̄íko	'rich'	pér̄a	'bitch'
krwél	'cruel'	kóro	'choir'	bérθa	'cabbage'
r̄ára	'rare'	péra	'pear'	onr̄áðo	'honest'
bárjos	'several'	kár̄o	'car'	enr̄ikeθér	'enrich'
ájre	'air'	bar̄ér	'sweep'	perðonár	'forgive'

10. HINDI
Focus: partial neutralization of the contrast between [s] and [š].

san	'year'	i:švar	'God'	bʰišti	'water-carrier'
šarad	'autumn'	kaš	'whip'	ra:ṣṭra	'country'
ṭe:ks	'tax'	iṣṭa	'desired'	duṣṭa	'wicked'
šan	'glory'	pakši	'bird'	suši:l	'well-bred'
gošt	'meat'	sasta	'cheap'	ce:ṣṭa	'attempt'
se:ṭʰ	'merchant'	do:sti	'friendship'	santuṣṭ	'satisfied'
vastu:	'stuff'	a:sma:n	'sky'	namaste:	'hello'

Unit I   45

11. WRITING PHONOLOGICAL RULES
Formalize the following statements. (N.B.: some require <u>two</u> rules, ordered.)

1. Voiceless stops are aspirated before a stressed vowel.
2. Liquids are voiceless after voiceless stops.
3. /t/ is voiceless before voiceless consonants, voiced before voiced consonants, and glottalized and voiceless word-finally.
4. Vowels become nasalized when before a nasal consonant.
5. Vowels become nasalized when adjacent to a nasal consonant.
6. When a consonant-initial ending is added to a stem ending in /h/, the /h/ drops.
7. Nasal consonants assimilate in point of articulation to a following consonant (assume that this language has only bilabial, alveolar, palatal, and velar consonants).
8. Postvocalic voiceless consonants become fricatives when followed by a stop, stops when followed by a fricative.
9. Rounded back vowels are fronted when a palatal glide or high front vowel follows in the next syllable. (Hint: "in the next syllable" is translated by allowing for any number of intervening consonants.)
10. Velars become palatals when before front vowels, uvulars when before mid or low back vowels.
11. Two successive vowels, whether within a word or within a phrase, are separated by the insertion of the glide [j].
12. /l/ velarizes postvocalically; it furthermore drops before a consonant, then leaving lip-rounding on the preceding vowel.
13. Alveolars are palatalized when before /j/; obstruents then become alveopalatal affricates, [nʲ] and [lʲ] become palatals, and [rʲ] becomes [ž].
14. When a vowel-initial ending is added to a consonant-final stem, that consonant exchanges position (metathesizes) with the vowel.
15. At the beginning of a phrase (i.e., when after a pause), fricatives are affricated.
16. Lax vowels are tensed word-finally, but all tense front vowels (including those which originate as lax vowels) take on a palatal glide when word-final.
17. Lax vowels are tensed word-finally, but all tense front vowels (excluding those which originate as lax vowels) take on a palatal glide when word-final.
18. All vowels are lengthened when before either a consonant and vowel or a vowel alone; but in lengthening, low vowels become mid.
19. When a prefix ending in [ə] precedes a consonant-initial stem, then the [ə] drops; the consonant preceding it in the prefix subsequently assimilates in voicing to the initial consonant of the stem.
20. If two adjacent syllables have high tone, the second drops to low tone.

12. NATURAL CLASSES

In each consonant or vowel system, some segments are circled. Determine whether these constitute a natural class within that system. If they do, give the shared features which define them as a natural class.

1. i (u)   2. i   u   3. (i ɯ) u   4. i (y) u   5. i y u
    e (o)   e   o   e ʌ o   e (ø) o   e (ø) o
    (a)   (æ a ɒ)   a   a   (æ œ)
                                                              a

6. (j w)   7. i   u   8. (i y) u   9. i (y u ɯ)   10. (i   u)
   (i u)   (e   o)   (e   o)   e (ø o ɣ)   (ɪ   ʊ)
    e o   (ɛ   ʌ)   (ɛ   ɔ)   a   e   o
    a   a   (a)   (ɛ ʌ ɔ)
                                                                a

11. (p) t k   12. p   t   k   13. p t k   14. p (c k)
    (b) d g   (b   d   g)   b d g   f (ç x)
    (f) s x   (f   θ   s)   (s)   h   m (ɲ ŋ)
        l   (ð   z)   (z)   l (ʎ)
                         r   l   w (j)
                     w

15. p t k   16. (p t k)   17. p t (č) k   18. p t k q
    b d g   (b d g)   b d (ǰ) g   (b d g G)
   (m n ŋ)   (ɸ s   x)   (f s)   r   (ɸ s x)
   (l   )   (z   )   (v z)   (m n)
   (r   )   (l ɬ)   r   (l)
                       w   l   R
                                        j

19. p (pʲ) t (tʲ) k (kʲ)   20. p   t č k   21. p t   k
    b   d   g   (ɸ   s   x)   v z   ɣ
    m   (n   ɲ)   (m   n   ŋ)   m n
    w   (r   j)   (l   )   l
          (ǰ)   (r   )
                               (ř   )   i u
                                    j   a

22. (p t) ts ʔ   23. p (t)   k ʔ   24. (p pʰ) (t tʰ) (k kʰ)
    (b d)   ɓ (ɗ)   (f)   (s)   (x)
    (θ) s   h   f (s š)   h   v   ð   ɣ
        m n   ŋ   (r)   n
                                                      l

25.
```
p  t  č  k
b  d  ǰ  g
f  s  š  x
v  z  ž
m  n
   l  ɨ
w
```
(circled: k, g, x, ž, ɨ, l, w)

26.
```
p  t  c  k
b  d  ɟ  g
ɸ  s     h
β  z  ɣ
   r
w     j
```
(circled: p t c k; s)

27.
```
p  p'  t  t'  k  k'  q  q'
b      d      g      ɢ
f      s
       l            tɬ'
       r
w
```
(circled: p p' t t' k k' q q'; tɬ')

13. **MARKING CONVENTIONS**
Ascertain which of the two segments in each pair is more natural, and write a marking convention for the feature(s) distinguishing them.

1. i ɯ	6. p pf	11. m ɱ	16. ɥ w
2. f ɸ	7. ɣ ʁ	12. š ç	17. z ʑ
3. s θ	8. c č	13. k x	18. e ø
4. r ř	9. a æ	14. ǰ dʲ	19. b ɓ
5. n ɲ	10. o ɤ	15. V Ṽ	20. m m̥

Now, working with sequences and positions, determine the relative naturalness of each set in the following pairs. (For the meaning of /, #, ___, etc., see the list of Generative Formalisms in the Introduction.)

21. /#____   (a): pt kt bg dv td cp
             (b): st ft sk zd vd šp

22. /#____   (a): ut ak ev ir ox æb
             (b): jt wk ɥv jr wx wb

23. /____#   (a): bn̩t dl̩d ptb gšq tβk sçt fθp
             (b): bn̩t dl̩d pəb gɔq tʊk sit fɯp

24. / V__V   (a): t k f x θ n̥ h
             (b): d g v ɣ ð n ɦ

25. /____‖   (a): t k f x θ n̥ h
             (b): d g v ɣ ð n ɦ

Unit II

Phonological Conditioning

Unit II

1. ITALIAN
Focus: [n], [ŋ] (Accents = stress.)

néro	'black'	njénte	'nothing'	dipínǰere	'depict'
sapóne	'soap'	úŋgja	'claw'	líŋgwa	'language'
bjáŋka	'white'	ónda	'wave'	téŋgo	'I have'
tornáre	'return'	stáŋko	'tired'	lúŋgo	'long'
ǰénte	'people'	invérno	'winter'	fíne	'end'
nónno	'grandfather'	dántsa	'dance'	frančéze	'French'
áŋke	'also'	fáŋgo	'mud'	kwantúŋkwe	'although'

2. DAGA
Focus: [s], [t]

jamosivin	'I am licking'	urase	'hole'	topen	'hit'
jamotain	'they will lick'	sinao	'drum'	use	'there'
asi	'grunt'	wagat	'holiday'	tave	'old'
anet	'we should go'	simura	'whisper'	siuran	'salt'
senao	'shout'	otu	'little'	tuian	'I kill'

3. OSSETIC
Focus: aspirated and unaspirated voiceless stops

tʰəχ	'strength'	kʰettag	'linen'	tʰas	'danger'
χesteg	'near'	eftən	'be added'	leppu	'boy'
fadatʰ	'possibility'	kʰasten	'I looked'	t̪sest	'eye'
kʰarkʰ	'hen'	akkag	'adequate'	dəkkag	'second'
t̪səppar	'four'	t̪sətʰ	'honor'	t̪səχt	'cheese'
kʰem	'where'	feste	'behind'	kʰom	'mouth'
pʰirən	'comb wool'	zaχta	'he told'	χeskard	'scissors'
		χeston	'military'	pʰerrest	'fluttering'

4. RUSSIAN
Focus: [i], [ɨ]   (Accents = stress.)

sudʲítʲ	'judge'	ptʲítsɨ	'birds'	ílʲi	'or'
bítʲ	'be'	vɨsókə	'high'	žɨná	'wife'
ískrə	'spark'	mɨ́lʲi	'they washed'	lʲáktʲi	'lie down!'
sɨtɨ	'sated'	sudɨ́	'courts'	kʲinó	'movie house'
jidá	'food'	rʲišɨtó	'sieve'	nɨ́l	'moaned'
xʲimʲík	'chemist'	bʲítʲ	'beat'	sʲílʲnə	'strongly'

5. AGUACATEC
Focus: voiced and voiceless liquids

l̥munč	'lemon'	tsontr̥	'against'	hobil	'knife'
tečl̥	'sign'	ʔuʔpl̥	'firecrackers'	lab	'ghost'
r̥meril	'hope'	bibl̥	'Bible'	teruʔ	'now'
wempl̥	'my ribs'	čerkš	'scissors'	balk	'brother-in-law'
bnol	'maker'	ploh	'useless'	qloʔ	'perhaps'
jol	'word'	s̥eluʔ	'your substitute'	l̥benuʔ	'you go'

6. PAPAGO
Focus: first, [t], [d], [č], and [ǰ]; second, the status of preconsonantal [h] and of voiceless nasals and vowels.

ǰihsk	'aunt'	daʔiwuhš	'run outside'	hɯhtahspčṵ	'make it five'
dɔʔak	'mountain'	ǰɯwɯhkɔh	'remove hair'	βaʔǰiwih	'swim'
ču:li̥	'corner'	ʔahidaʔk	'year'	ǰu:ʔw̥	'rabbits'
čɯβaʔgi̥	'clouds'	dɔhaʔihčuhk	'will be anything'	hɯǰɯli̥	'self'
βahču̥m	'drown, dive'	čɯhči̥	'name'	stɔḁ	'white'
taht	'foot'	ǰumali̥	'low'	čihkpan	'work'
ʔi:da	'this'	tɔnɔm̥	'be thirsty'	stahtɔnɔm:ah	'thirsty times'
mɯɯ̥dam	'runner'	ntɔçi̥	'I'll go'	piwɯhɔ	'not true'

Unit II
                                                                                53

7. ZULU
   Focus: [e], [ɛ]; [o], [ɔ]. Your analysis should be valid regardless of length.
          (Tone omitted; accents = stress.)

àɓelú:si	'herdsman'	ɓɔ́:na	'see'	ɛndɮɛlé:ni	'in the path'
ló:lu	'this'	isí:mɔ	'shape'	ɬàɓɛlé:la	'sing'
u:ʇé:zu	'slice'	ɛlá:kʰɛ	'his'	ùmlɔ́:mɔ	'mouth'
iňó:ni	'bird'	ʇé:da	'finish'	i:t'wé:t'we	'apprehension'
ezí:ňɛ	'others'	i:ɮé:lɔ	'pasture'	boɗú:la	'pull out of mud'
ɓoɓí:sa	'worry'	ɓɔ́:ɓa	'relate'	nɛʇɔ́:la	'and the wagon'

8. AMHARIC
   Focus: [ɛ], [ʌ]

fʌllʌgʌ	'he wanted'	gʌnzʌb	'money'	lačč'ɛ	'he shaved'
fʌrʌs	'horse'	k'ažžɛ	'talked in his sleep'	žele	'unarmed'
tʌnʌsa	'stand up!'	ǰɛgna	'brave'	aššɛ	'he rubbed'
jɛlɨǰlɨǰ	'grandchild'	nʌɲ	'I am'	jɛllum	'no'
agʌɲɲɛ	'he found'	mʌwdʌd	'to like'	šemmʌggʌlʌ	'he became old'
tʌmʌččɛ	'it got comfortable'	žemmʌrʌ	'he started'	bʌk'k'ʌlʌ	'it germinated'
majɛt	'see'	mʌnnʌsat	'get up'	mʌst'ʌt	'give'
mokkʌrʌ	'he tried'	mʌmkʌr	'advise'	mʌč	'when'

9. ARAWAK
   Focus: [o], [u] (Accents = stress.)

tʰokóro	'her knee'	lobána	'his liver'	úri	'snake'
ɸírotʰo	'it's big'	nakábu	'they're bathing'	pámu	'salt'
bubúra	'for you'	ɸámu	'lying face down'	somúle	'drunk'
dakóna	'my thumb'	horóro	'earth'	dakóši	'my eyes'
namúda	'they climb up'	úɲi	'rain'	waɸúda	'we blow'

10. FRENCH
(a) Focus: [m], [m̥], [l], [l̥], [r] (=[ʀ]), [r̥] (=[ʀ̥])

rəlir	'reread'	fɛrm	'fixed'	ɛtr̥	'be'
plɛr	'please'	kadr	'framework'	pœpl̥	'people'
myr	'wall'	nɛgr	'black'	sjɛkl̥	'century'
rar	'rare'	marbr	'marble'	šapitr̥	'chapter'
il	'island'	fɛbl	'weak'	krwatr̥	'grow'
bœr	'butter'	bɛrl	'water-parsnip'	prism̥	'prism'
tɛl	'such'	djabl	'devil'	tripl̥	'triple'
tɛr	'land'	kɥivr	'copper'	bukl̥	'brooch'
lim	'file'	film	'film'	spasm̥	'spasm'
ɛme	'love'	paradigm	'paradigm'	sufl̥	'puff of air'
surir	'smile'	surdr	'gush'	sufr̥	'sulfur'

(b) In colloquial Parisian French, [ʀ] and [ʀ̥] have become fricatives, [ʁ] and [χ]. Assume the above data have fricatives instead of trills. What generalization is still present underlyingly which is not obvious in phonetic representation?

11. TSWANA
(a) Focus: [d], [l]   (Accents = tone.)

lèfìfì	'darkness'	xòɲálà	'marry'	lòkwálɔ̀	'letter'
lòlémè	'tongue'	léŋ	'when'	kʰúdù	'tortoise'
sèlépè	'axe'	lòxàdìmá	'lightning flash'	mòsádí	'woman'
mòlɔ̀mò	'mouth'	dìjɔ́	'food'	pódì	'goat'
xòbàlà	'read'	m̩màdì	'reader'	bàdísá	'the herd'
lèrúmɔ̀	'spear'	dùmélà	'greetings'		

(b) Given your analysis of [l] above, how would you account for its occurrence in the clusters below? (Hint: must it be a separate segment?)

xòtlà	'come'	n̩tlò	'house'	-tlìlé	'we came'
tlàlà	'hunger'	sèntlè	'well'	-útlúlé	'heard'

Unit II

12. CATALAN
Focus: [b], [b:], [β]; [g], [g:], [γ] (Accents = stress.)

tríb:lə	'triple'	gέr̄ə	'war'	pób:lə	'town'
dəšéb:lə	'disciple'	əγrəðá	'please'	úŋg:lə	'fingernail'
əmbέžə	'envy'	kámbi	'change'	r̄ég:lə	'rule'
bárβə	'beard'	əmərγó	'bitterness'	téβə	'your'
bén	'wind'	frέγə	'he scrubs'	ség:lə	'century'
ɲəβít	'gulf'	ub:lít	'forgetfulness'	kuβárt	'coward'
ərtíg:lə	'article'	təmbé	'also'	fərβén	'boiling'
səŋgunós	'bloodied'	béwrə	'drink'		

13. PIPIL
Focus: [t], [t']; [ł], [l]

nakat'	'meat'	taštawa	'pay'	tuši	'intestine'
titwiz	'you come'	wiłut'	'dove'	takat'	'man'
ihsatuk	'awake'	istit'	'fingernail'	tehtečan	'people'
lamat'	'old lady'	tihłan	'hen'	kałat'	'frog'
piłtsin	'boy'	komatoł	'rainbow'	kał	'house'
ličihčiuka	'decorate'				

14. PENNSYLAVANIA GERMAN
Focus: [r] (=[r̄]) and [ʁ] (Accents = stress.)

rót	'red'	tíʁ	'door'	nóxpəʁ	'neighbor'
šrájβə	'write'	tírə	'doors'	kárəp	'basket'
βáʁšt	'sausage'	márɪk	'market'	krúmpɪʁ	'potato'
máʁ	'mare'	réjərə	'rain'	páwraj	'farm'
štrós	'street'	krót	'toad'	márə	'mares'
ríŋə	'rings'				

15. ARABELA
(a) Focus: nasalized and non-nasalized vowels and glides. (Stress omitted.)

sowaka?	'wall'	suro?	'monkey'	nĩĩkjææ̃?	'is pouring out'
suwaka?	'type of fish'	mjæ̃nũ?	'swallow'	nẽẽkjææ̃?	'lying on its back'
mõnũ?	'kill'	tukuru?	'palm leaf'	njææ̃ri?	'he laid it down'
nĩtjænũ?	'carry on back'	šijokwa?	'grease'	posunãha?	'short person'
kuwɔxo?	'hole'	nõõnũ?	'be pained'	nãnãã?	'he's bathing'
tæwe?	'foreigner'	mããnũ?	'woodpecker'	hjuuššænõ?	'where I fished'

(b) Status of glottal stop: is it distinctive or redundant?

16. SPANISH
Focus: [s], [z] (Accents = stress.)

(a)
esféra	'sphere'	sésos	'brains'	mízmo	'same'
kastíθo	'pure'	kásas	'houses'	ízla	'island'
asustár	'frighten'	píso	'floor'	áznos	'asses'
péska	'he fishes'	kási	'almost'	ezβélto	'slender'
r̄úsos	'Russians'	késo	'cheese'	r̄ázɣo	'feature'
lósas	'tiles'	desjérto	'desert'	dézðe	'since'

(b)
las kásas	'the houses'	laz lósas	'the tiles'
las ízlas	'the islands'	laz βákas	'the cows'

17. TUCANO
Focus: plain and prenasalized voiced stops. (Accents = tones.)

ᵐbì?í	'mouse'	etágù	'the one who's arriving'	ᵐbè?ró	'afterwards'
págàh	'stomach'	ⁿdìá	'river'	ⁿdàsé	'toucan'
ᵐbù?ú	'type of fish'	kà?bí	'soft'	ⁿdìájùh	'dog'
ᵐbù?édàh	'rainbow'	ⁿdíh	'blood'	ⁿdì?tá	'earth'
ᵐbù?besé	'injection'				

Unit II

18. TAGALOG
Focus: [k], [x]

ʌxɔ	'I'	wiːxʌʔ	'language'	sʌklɪt	'hook'
ʔuːlʌk	'reel'	tuːxɔd	'cane'	baːxɪt	'why'
kʌʔɔn	'fetch'	mʌxʌrɪnɪg	'hear'	kwaːgɔh	'owl'
kowntɪʔ	'a little'	sʊxʌ	'vinegar'	maːskɔt	'mascot'
kʌmɪh	'we'				

19. CAMPA
Focus: [ɛ], [e]; [ɪ], [i] (Accents = stress.)

etíni	'armadillo'	nihánda	'far away'	oaríntsi	'roasted meat'
ɪŋgáni	'rain'	tapétsa	'vine'	íiri	'his nose'
nojéa	'I eat'	ɪɲáhi	'his bill'	pókite	'cook it!'
pitíro	'cockroach'	šiɛ́ndi	'dragonfly'	nombakotémbi	'I'll show you'

20. CATALAN
(a) Focus: [a], [æ], [aˀ], [ə] (Accents = stress.)

kámə	'leg'	əsǽžə	'he tries'	fáˀɫs	'ravine'
ʎástimə	'pity'	trəβǽʎ	'work'	káˀɫp	'bald'
fáŋ	'mud'	kǽšə	'box'	bláˀw	'blue'
márə	'mother'	əfǽŋ	'eagerness'	kláˀw	'nail'
žərmá	'brother'	mǽj	'never'	dizβáˀwšə	'excess'
gát	'cat'	mǽč	'May'	məláˀɫ	'ill'

(b) Focus: [l], [ɫ], using above and following data.

pɛ́ɫ	'hair'	míɫ	'thousand'	móɫdrə	'grind'
əskóɫtə	'he listens'	kóɫzə	'elbow'	ləktúrə	'reading'
álə	'wing'	bílə	'village'	bulé	'want'

21. HAUSA
Focus: labialized and palatalized velars and labials. (Accents = tones.)

bʷùɓú:	'sack'	ɓʷóːjèː	'hide'	kÀrɓáː	'receive'
gÁníː	'see'	kʷúɗíː	'money'	sáːbʷóː	'new'
k'ÁlÁw	'very'	kʷúnnéː	'ear'	k'ʷóːɸàː	'doorway'
ɓʷúntúː	'rice-husks'	bàːkʲíː	'mouth'	kʲéː	'you'
kʲírkʲìː	'excellence'	báːkʷúnàː	'mouths'	ɗÀwkʲéː	'take'
kʷòːjóː	'learn'	gʷòːbɛ́	'tomorrow'	gʲíɗáː	'house'
k'Àršéː	'end'	gÁbÀs	'east'	kÀréː	'dog'
léːɓèː	'lip'	kʷúsÁ	'near'	bíjú	'two'
sÁwk'ʲíː	'ease'	káːtáːkʷóː	'lumber'	lóːkÀčíː	'time'
báːjæː	'back'	gʷùmíː	'sweat'	kʷúllúm	'every day'
k'áːrèː	'finish'	k'ʷùndúː	'gizzard'	k'ʷòːk'Àríː	'worthy effort'
bÁŋgʷóː	'wall'	bìskʲít	'cookie'	dÀgÀ	'from'

22. SIRIONO
Focus: first, [b] and [β], [d] and [ð]; second, [p] [ɸ] and [pʰ], [t] [θ] and [tʰ], [k] and [kʰ]; third, consonantal lengthening. (Accents = stress.)

dipːikíːəsːu	'large yam'	kiríðːia	'wind'	erȭð̃ːí	'dirty'
áβːitːurə	'good grand-mother'	emːū̃βːe	'make a road'	ẽbːaásːa	'he does'
béo	'fly'	deðːéa	'small palm'	ɨβːíɨ	'below'
déu	'thigh'	ninːíβːu	'spit'	sedːaǰːá	'stingray'
eiðːóahːe	'kill with a club'	emːitːirõiðːía	'not clear'		
íːke	'child'	ɲéθːe	'small'	tausːíə	'excrement'
pʰée	'far away'	pəmːəi	'angry'	čúɲːo	'believe'
kʰárə	'was'	taɨrásːi	'I sing'	kisːíkːui	'squirrel'
níɸːi	'sweet potato'	čeásːu	'wild pig'	ẽ̄gːəθːũ̄ɨ̃	'tapir'
tʰáθːa	'fire'	hẽ̄íθːe	'top of the head'	katːugːúθːi	'left side'
gúθːi	'toward'	teahːíri	'acquainted'	eakːáθːu	'know'

Unit II

23. GONJA
    Focus: [m], [m̩], [n], [n̩], [ɲ], [ɲ̩], [ŋ], [ŋ̩], [r], [r̩]. (Accents = tone.)

ń̩sá	'wine'	èkpàmpò	'hunter'	ní	'if'
ǹ̩dó	'farm'	àgb͡íɲén	'wizard'	ɲí	'know'
ŋ̩́kú	'oil'	g͡bìŋ	'big'	n̩térí	'yesterday'
ŋ̩g͡bŕ̩	'language'	fóŋ	'blow'	mòŋúlómbì	'oval'
ǹ̩sàpàpŕ̩	'pito'	púnté	'shout'	dàmàtá	'many'
m̩fé	'here'	ɲcú	'water'	nàwòlè	'alone'
èléŋ	'strength'	kámé	'a duck'	ɲɔ́	'dye'
áɲénpé	'boss'	káŋé	'say'	kìkúmú	'heart'
kìlàmfɛ̀	'horn'	kúr	'dig'	ɲcɛ́r	'long ago'
ḿ̩fól	'salt'	br̩	'bring'	ɲàŋáràŋ	'rough'
ń̩sónɛ̀	'ash'	ǹdúɲ	'there'	léŋlèrì	'now'
mɔ̀	'kill'	ǹnà	'this'	pìlìɲcímbì	'short'

24. OLD NORSE
    (a) Focus: [g], [ɟ], [k], [c]. (Accents = stress.)

ɟéva	'give'	ɟíl	'ravine'	ɟœra	'make'
hríŋgr	'ring'	ɟjóf	'gift'	cjó:za	'choose'
gó:ðr	'good'	éjci	'oak timber'	cý:r	'cow'
kóna	'wife'	gárpr	'gallant fel-low'	ɟævr	'mild'
kró:kr	'hook'	gúma	'man'	æɟir	'the sea'
dráɣa	'pull'	dáɣr	'day'	bjárɣ	'rock'
hní:ɣa	'sink'	bóɟi	'bow'	séɟja	'say'
kúnninɟi	'acquaintance'	cæra	'accuse'	á:ɟæti	'glory'
círcja	'church'	kʊttr	'cat'	ká:tr	'merry'
kβíðliŋgr	'ditty'	θáɣall	'silent'	náɣl	'nail'
láwɣ	'bath'	réka	'drive'	gnó:ɣr	'enough'

(b) Focus: [g], [ɟ], [ɣ]

25. SWAHILI
Focus: implosive and explosive voiced stops and affricates.

ɓeɓa	'carry on the back'	ŋgapi	'how many'	ndefu	'long'
ɗamu	'blood'	haɓari	'news'	ɟeŋga	'build'
ɟembe	'hoe'	ndeɠe	'bird'	ňǰema	'good'
mbovu	'rotten'	mgaŋga	'medicine man'	ɓeɠa	'shoulder'
puňǰe	'kernel'	ɓaɗo	'not yet'	fuŋga	'fasten'
ɠiza	'darkness'	ɲekundu	'red'	ndizi	'banana'
mfereɟi	'ditch'	mbaja	'bad'		

26. ATSUGEWI
Focus: tense and lax non-low vowels. (Accents = tone.)

(a)
ɪskí:čanwo	'few'	čɔtwajá	'chipmunk'	čɪqwatəwa:	'push'
nariji:	'trout'	ʊtstájwoho	'near'	wɪssu:	'blow'
maxči	'fish'	tʔɔxqʔa:	'raccoon'	rə́ksehí:	'name'
pokuwɪtswa	'swell'	póxom	'hemlock'	qíwinʊssa	'freeze'
mɪkhtte	'flint'	čiwohó	'other'	tsílulɪts	'large'
wɔstawá	'spit'	mahkú	'deer'	čučkí:	'foot'
halʊpkajwá	'snake'	čɛxtə	'brown ant'	qɔtsəkpátshɛtsne	'that's the man who did it'

(b)
loʔpupía	'fern'	mitiʔjé:	'turn'		
čineʔwó:	'sun'	súʔkahaw	'owl'	ɪssiníwɪʔnka	'Red Hill'

(c) In view of your analysis for (a), how would you analyze long [n:] in:

wʊn:uwi	'cotton-topped tule'	tɛwtewɪn:i	'salmon flies'

(d) Could [ts] be analyzed as a single segment, affricate /t͜s/, in this language?

27. CHAMA
Focus: voiced and voiceless vowels and nasals. (Accents = stress.)

xá	'parrot'	xaxasí	'post'	eŋḁ́ŋo̥	'tail'
exá	'egg'	óxe̥	'river'	ejáho̥	'above'
čóčo̥	'headgear'	ʔíni̥	'bee'	šáni̥	'right side'
ŋókʷi̥	'sit down!'	éxḁ	'people'	eoxʷḁ́ŋḁ	'scalp'

Unit II

28. QUECHUA
Focus: [i], [e], [u], [o]

(a)
qori	'gold'	čoχlu	'corn on the cob'	q'omir	'green'
niŋri	'ear'	moqo	'runt'	hoq'ara	'deaf'
pʰuʎu	'blanket'	jujaŋ	'he recalls'	tuʎu	'bone'
api	'take'	suti	'name'	oɴqoj	'be sick!'
čilwi	'baby chick'	čʰičiŋ	'he whispers'	qečuŋ	'he disputes it'
p'isqo	'bird'	musoχ	'new'	čuŋka	'ten'
čuʎu	'ice'	qʰeʎa	'lazy'	čeqaŋ	'straight'

(b) Focus: [k], [q], [x], [χ], [ŋ], [ɴ], using above and following data.

qaŋ	'you'	noqa	'I'	čaxra	'field'
čeχniŋ	'he hates'	soχta	'six'	aχna	'thus'
ʎixʎa	'small shawl'	qosa	'husband'	qara	'skin'
alqoχ	'dog'	seɴqa	'nose'	karu	'far'
atoχ	'fox'	qaŋkuna	'you (pl.)'	pusaχ	'eight'
č'aki	'dry'	wateχ	'again'	waχtaj	'hit'
haku	'let's go'	waqaj	'tears'	kaŋka	'roasted'
tʰakaj	'drop'	waleχ	'good, well'	waxča	'poor'

29. SCOTS (CONSERVATIVE)
Focus: [ø], [ʏ]

gʏd	'good'	møzɪk	'music'	šø	'shoe'
dø	'do'	frʏt	'fruit'	šʏn	'shoes'
dʏn	'done'	blʏd	'blood'	pør	'poor'
fʏl	'fool'	kʏt	'ankle'	jʏs	'use (noun)'
spʏn	'spoon'	rʏf	'roof'	jøz	'use (verb)'
blʏm	'bloom'	jʏθ	'youth'	prøv	'prove'
børd	'board'	bʏk	'book'	_____	'proof'

30. ZUÑI
Focus: position of stress; [x], [h]; [a], [æ], [k], [kʲ]; and the underlying representation of glottalized consonants.

ʔaníktoha	'meet'	liʔk'óhanna	'dime'	leháʔpa	'certainly'
hajtóšnaːwe	'customs'	texjá	'be valued'	hoʔʔí	'he's alive'
ʔexwánne	'crotch'	wexkʲǽ	'Eastern Keres'	heʔšó	'chewing gum'
jeːláxše	'let's run'	ʔexkʷí	'be first'	kʷaʔkʷíxʔamme	'it is not spilled'
jaɫápkʲæ	'they asked him'	tewɫášši	'kind person'	kʲækʷ'án	'at the house'
číppá	'it's coarse'	makʲkʲí	'woman with children'	ɫemkʲ'ǽjanne	'ice'
ʔaːkú	'purple sage'	ʔampísa	'be hyperactive'	ɫajáːluk'o	'valley bluebird'
kʲemmé	'leather'	k'okší	'be good'	tamsákʲæjanna	'be naked'
ʔaktsékʲ'i	'boy, son'	kʲ'iɫkʲǽ	'it got hot'	paɫt'á	'at the end'
ʔisk'ón	'near there'	tsittá	'mother'	suskʲí	'coyote'
ʔanʔélumʔa	'he likes it'	lup'é	'box of ashes'	patč'ápa	'kinglet'
ɫašš'á	'he's getting old'	ʔeɫé	'corpse'	ʔojʔó	'mourn'
siʔkʲænne	'unkempt person'	ʔank'ókši	'be tame'	ʔipéʔku	'stumble'

31. ARAUCANIAN
Focus: [ɸ], [β], [θ], [ð], [š], [č]. (Accents = tones.)

θómo	'woman'	θuŋúlàn	'I don't speak'	kɯθáw	'work'
βuʈá	'big'	tɯɸáči	'that'	sánšu	'pig'
kɯðáw	'work'	čáo	'father'	píši	'small'
ɸóro	'bone'	ɸuʈá	'big'	tɯβáči	'that'
píči	'small'	ðómo	'woman'	βóro	'bone'
šáo	'father'	sánču	'pig'	ðuŋúlàn	'I don't speak'
tɯɸáši	'that'	tɯβáši	'that'		

Unit II 63

32. SPANISH (CASTILIAN)
(a) Focus: nasals (Accents = stress; <u>t</u> and <u>d</u> represent dentals everywhere; <u>r̄</u> is alveolar.)

káma	'bed'	límpjo	'clean'	káɲa	'cane'
óṇθa	'ounce'	káŋa	'white hair'	eṇθía	'gums'
óṇda	'wave'	fiŋxír	'pretend'	eɱférmo	'sick'
beŋgáṇθa	'vengeance'	beṇtáxa	'advantage'	ámbos	'both'
gáñčo	'hook'	óṇr̄a	'honor'	kaṇtáṇdo	'sing'
iɱfjérno	'hell'	θíŋko	'five'	pensáron	'they thought'
kóñča	'shell'	moṇtón	'pile'	koɱfesár	'confess'

(b)

eŋ kanaðá	'in Canada'	koŋ xwán	'with John'
em beneθwéla	'in Venezuela'	koṇ djéɣo	'with James'
eñ číle	'in Chile'	kon alfónso	'with Alphonse'
en arxeṇtína	'in Argentina'	koɱ fernándo	'with Fred'
___ fráṇθja	'in France'	___ páβlo	'with Paul'

(c–h) Focus: voiced stops and fricatives

(c)

óŋgos	'mushrooms'	imbjérno	'winter'	látiɣo	'whip'
seɣír	'follow'	dwéṇde	'elf'	múṇdo	'world'
kwéβa	'cave'	krúðo	'raw'	aβoɣáðo	'lawyer'
lúmbre	'light'	r̄wéða	'wheel'	areŋgáβa	'was haranguing'

(d)

gér̄a	'war'	kerúβ	'cherub'	síɣlo	'century'
duðár	'doubt'	boṇdáð	'goodness'	aðxetíβo	'adjective'
bómba	'pump'	θiɣθáɣ	'zigzag'	díɣno	'worthy'
gáŋga	'bargain'	birtúð	'virtue'	oβtéŋgo	'I get'
bwéḻto	'returned'	θéspeð	'yard'	óðre	'wineskin'

(e)

árβol	'tree'	atizβár	'pry into'	arɣwír	'argue'
r̄ázɣo	'feature'	aʎáθɣo	'discovery'	dézðe	'since'
aðβertír	'warn'				

CONTINUED →

(32. SPANISH, CONTINUED)

(f)
kolɣár	'hang'	álɣo	'something'	umíl̪de	'humble'
kálβo	'bald'	fál̪da	'skirt'	búlβo	'bulb'
tól̪do	'awning'	al̪déa	'village'	alβaɲíl	'mason'

(g)

	'day'	'cat'	'boat'
(in isolation)	día	gáto	bárko
'the...'	el̪ día	el ɣáto	el βárko
'a...'	un̪ día	uŋ gáto	um bárko
'every...'	káða ðía	káða ɣáto	káða βárko
'two...'	doz ðías	doz ɣátos	doz βárkos

(h) You may have noted by now that [l] and [l̪] never contrast---the latter occurs only before dentals. In at least one solution for this exercise, the <u>l</u>-dentalization rule is ordered with respect to the extended rule for sections (c-h).

33. KOREAN
    Focus: [l], [ll], [r], [lʲ].

(a)
ratio	'radio'	nolla	'play!'	pʰalʲman	'80,000'
rupi	'ruby'	mʌlli	'far off'	čalʲmos	'mistake'
aræ	'below'	tal	'moon'	aːlʲm	'knowledge'
iri	'this way'	kul	'orange'	kalʲbi	'ribs'
tʌrʌ	'publication'	kumul	'net'	čʰilʲjo	'medical treatment'
kɯræ	'yes'	tʰʌl	'hair'		

(b) Focus: [s], [sʲ]

sʲi	'poem'	sul	'wine'	sʲy	'soon'
son	'hand'	čʌpsʲi	'plate'	suto	'capital'
sæ	'bird'	sʲypke	'easily'	sø	'iron'
mas	'flavor'	sʲijem	'exam'	suŋkaŋki	'elevator'

Unit II   65

34. MARGI
Focus: [a], [æ], [ɔ], [œ], [u], [y]. (Accents = tones.)

šýná	'despise'	fúr	'buffalo'	šǽɗá	'reply'
sóró	'rectangular mud house'	ɉylía	'surround'	žæ̀ɓí	'cloth'
cæ̀r	'tongue'	dzábá	'measure'	ùçì	'guinea corn'
sɔ̀sɔ́	'sponge'	ɦùmù	'plentiful'	jǽɗí	'millet'
šæšílgà	'star'	xùmbù	'armpit'	čỳɗǘ	'stir'
ndɔ̀lá	'throw into'	ɉykùr	'love'	úfwážỳɗù	'wild cat'
mádóɗú	'gall'	çæ̀vòlì	'type of fish'	kúɓǘ	'manure'
ɲæ̀ní	'fill'	bàbál	'open place'	ɉæmbál	'curved sword'
zúŋ	'straight'	čæ̀čæ̀ɗǘ	'chosen'	ɬànà	'cut off'
çæ̀çœ́ɗà	'fish'	ɉærmá	'brown guinea corn'	jæ̀jæ̀	'fruit'

35. OLD NORSE
Focus: [θ], [ð], [d], [f], [v], [b], [β]; is there more than one solution?

ferð	'journey'	hav	'sea'	duɣa	'help'
βatn	'water'	javn	'equal'	draɣa	'pull'
blanda	'mix'	βið	'toward'	saɣði	'said'
faðir	'father'	θurva	'need'	θjoːð	'people'
froːðr	'wise'	θoːvi	'saddle-pad'	biða	'await'
βaða	'wade'	baːðir	'both'	βaːndr	'difficult'
dauði	'death'	daːð	'energy'	kljuva	'cleave'
fen	'bog'	βevr	'web'	θβeŋgr	'thong'
θaðan	'thence'	βerða	'happen'	θreivaðumk	'I groped'

36. ENGLISH
Focus: [t], [d] between [n] and sibilant.

sɪnts	'since'	awnts	'ounce'	brandz	'bronze'
wʌnts	'once'	tʰɛnts	'tense'	pʰændzi	'pansy'
æntsɚ	'answer'	dæntsɪŋ	'dancing'	bənændzə	'bonanza'
hɛnts	'hence'	rɪnts	'rinse'	mindz	'means'

37. JAPANESE

(a) Focus: [t], [d], [ts], [dz], [č], [ǰ], [s], [š], [z]

ása	'morning'	haší	'bridge'	mudzukašii	'is difficult'
asá	'flax'	hadzu	'expectation'	mačiaišitsu	'waiting room'
áraši	'storm'	henǰi	'reply'	ráǰio	'radio'
betsu	'separate'	hodo	'extent'	suni	'afterwards'
čičí	'father'	konšjuu	'this week'	sensée	'teacher'
čjawan	'cup'	kusá	'grass'	tottemo	'very'
daibu	'many'	kuší	'cloth'	zéçi	'by all means'
dénuči	'exit'	kjoǰin	'giant'	zonǰínai	'don't know'
doitsuno	'German (language)'	kutsu	'shoes'	zaidan	'foundation'
dóozo	'please'	ǰitenšja	'bicycle'	dzubon	'trousers'
geešja	'geisha'	pénči	'pliers'	šidzuka	'quiet'
hadé	'gaudy'	rendzu	'lens'	šjoou	'soy sauce'
háši	'chopsticks'	sooǰi	'cleaning'	ǰjanuči	'faucet'

(b) Focus: [h], [ɸ], [b], [p], [m], [n], [w], [g], [ŋ], [k], [ç], using above and following data.

ban	'night'	góhan	'cooked rice'	káŋu	'furniture'
burásu	'blouse'	gasorin	'gasoline'	nawá	'rope'
bjooki	'sick'	gun	'county'	ɸuhee	'complaint'
wan	'bowl'	gjuniku	'beef'	ɸutatsu	'two units'
çíbači	'brazier'	háha	'mother'	naiɸu	'knife'
çiŋaší	'east'	hóoku	'fork'	oɸúro	'bath'
çjaku	'100'	kani	'crab'	pan	'bread'
čiŋáu	'is wrong'	kamí	'paper'	rippa	'magnificent'
eeŋo	'English (language)'	kámi	'top'	úmi	'sea'
enrjo	'restraint'	kaŋí	'key'	kannan	'hardship'

(c) The acute accent represents a combination of stress and the falling of sustained pitch. Is pitch/stress distinctive in Japanese?
(d) Is the syllabicity of [n] predictable?
(e) Is there any evidence that might motivate a reanalysis of the phoneme /u/?

Unit II

38. MODERN GREEK

(a) Focus: voiced and voiceless fricatives and stops. (Accents = stress; the symbol ñ represents a brief nasal (homorganic to the following consonant) which can optionally be deleted.)

blé	'blue'	ðrómos	'road'	próeðros	'president'
γnósis	'knowledge'	ísixos	'quiet'	grízos	'gray'
blúza	'blouse'	ksanθós	'blond'	vómva	'bomb'
akáθartos	'dirty'	bárñbas	'uncle'	dropalós	'bashful'
ðjáðoxos	'crown prince'	dinó	'I get dressed'	závγos	'pair'
krívo	'I hide'	áñdras	'man'	arγá	'late'
prézvis	'ambassador'	laðí	'oil'	piγúni	'chin'
vléma	'glance'	kliðóno	'I lock'	fakós	'lens'
brávo	'well done'	kañbína	'cabin'	bakális	'grocer'
gremnós	'precipice'	várvaros	'barbarian'	ðíno	'I give'
ðíki	'lawsuit'	demoñdé	'old-fashioned'	páñdos	'at any rate'
tíxi	'fate'	vaθmós	'degree'	lañbrós	'bright'
áñgelos	'messenger'	ðáða	'torch'	eñgríno	'I approve'
xoñdrós	'coarse'	eñgéfalos	'brain'	drépomai	'I'm ashamed'
kóvo	'I cut'	aγapó	'I love'	komfós	'elegant'
garsóni	'waiter'	vréxi	'it's raining'	plevrá	'side'
buzí	'sparkplug'	añgúri	'cucumber'	aðjávroxo	'raincoat'
karfítsa	'brooch'	extés	'yesterday'	káθetos	'vertical'
kéfi	'humor'	xartí	'paper'	tútos	'this'

(b) How might the following data affect your analysis? (ton = 'the', masculine accusative singular; tin = 'the', feminine accusative singular.)

kafé	('coffee')	toñgafé	piní	('punishment')	tiñbiní
kólpos	('bay')	toñgólpo	páli	('struggle')	tiñbáli
táfos	('tomb')	toñdáfo	tráγos	('goat')	toñdráγo
kíknos	('swan')	toñgíkno	áñdras	('man')	tonáñdras
város	('weight')	tomváro			

Unit III

Grammatical Conditioning

Unit III

1. GERMAN
   Focus: [x], [ç]

(a)
láːxən	'laugh'	kRíːçt	'crawls'	nóx	'still'
zúːxt	'looks for'	pʰéç	'bad luck'	býːçəR	'books'
hóːx	'high'	míç	'me'	báx	'brook'
áwx	'also'	lǿçəR	'holes'	meçáːnik	'mechanics'
lájçt	'easy'	fáwxən	'spitting'	kʰoːxəm	(place-name)
óyç	'you (pl.)'	zíçt	'vision'	búxt	'inlet'

(b)
mǿnç	'monk'	ɛ́lç	'elk'	dúRç	'through'
dólç	'dagger'	mánçə	'many a'	çemíː	'chemistry'
çíːna	'China'	çiRúRk	'surgeon'		

(c)
| kʰuː | 'cow' | pfáw | 'peacock' | foːtoːçemíː | 'photochemistry' |
| kʰuːçən | 'little cow' | pfáwçən | 'little peacock' | | |

2. DUTCH
   Focus: variation in the formation of the diminutive.

	noun	diminutive		noun	diminutive
(a) 'egg'	æj	æjcə	'door'	døːr	døːrcə
'son'	zoːn	zoːncə	'blanket'	deːkən	deːkəncə
'spoon'	leːpəl	leːpəlcə	'cow'	kuː	kuːcə
(b) 'bag'	zak	zakjə	'book'	buːk	buːkjə
'letter'	briːf	briːfjə	'ship'	sxɪp	sxɪpjə
'tree'	boːm	boːmpjə	'thumb'	dœym	dœympjə
'arm'	arm	armpjə			
(c) 'house'	hœys	hœyšə	'cat'	kat	kacə
'boat'	boːt	boːcə	'glass'	glaːs	glaːšə
'razor'	sxeːrməs	sxeːrməšə	'box'	doːs	_____
			'quarter'	kvart	_____

3. SHONA
Focus: formation of the passive, and accompanying alternations.

		basic verb	passive		basic verb	passive
(a)	'cook'	-ɓika	-ɓikwa	'leave'	-rega	-regwa
	'bind'	-suŋga	-suŋgwa	'growl'	-oŋa	-oŋwa
	'beg'	-pemha	-pemhwa	'reap'	-koha	-kohwa
(b)	'capture'	-tapa	-tapxa	'dip'	-diba	-dibɣa
	'play'	-tamba	-tambɣa	'bite'	-ruma	-rumŋa
(c)	'omit'	-rova	-rovɣʷa	'hold'	-ɓata	-ɓatxʷa
	'mount'	-gada	-gadɣʷa	'lose'	-rasa	-rasxʷa
	'carve'	-βeza	-βezɣʷa	'hunt'	-kʷaša	-kʷašxʷa
	'barter'	-šuža	-šužɣʷa	'roast'	-goča	-gočxʷa
	'leak'	-ǰuǰa	-ǰuǰɣʷa	'amuse'	-setsa	_____
(d)	'love'	-ɗa	-ɗiwa	'give'	-pa	-piwa
	'steal'	-ɓa	-ɓiwa	'eat'	-ẖa	-ẖiwa
	'fear'	-ɬa	-ɬiwa			

(e) How is the following deviant? 'go out' -ɓuɗa -ɓuɗwa

4. KOREAN
Focus: consonant alternations in verb stems

		infinitive	plain present		infinitive	plain present
(a)	'wear shoes'	sinʌ	sinnɯnta	'listen'	tɯlʌ	tɯnnɯnta
	'close'	tatʌ	tannɯnta	'get better'	naːsʌ	naːnnɯnta
	'comb'	pisʌ	pinnɯnta	'follow'	čočʰʌ	čonnɯnta
	'find'	čʰačʌ	čʰannɯnta			
(b)	'wear'	ipʌ	imnɯnta	'help'	toːwʌ	toːmnɯnta
	'eat'	mʌkʌ	mʌŋnɯnta	'polish'	tak̄ʌ	taŋnɯnta

Unit III

5. PORTUGUESE

(a) Focus: stem alternations between [o] and [ɔ]. (Accents = stress.)

	m. sg.	m. pl.	f. sg.	f. pl.
'fire'	fógu	fóguš		
'people'	póvu	póvuš		
'eye'	óʎu	óʎuš		
'new'	nóvu	nóvuš	nɔ́va	nɔ́vaš
'dead'	mórtu	mórtuš	mɔ́rta	mɔ́rtaš
'famous'	famózu	famózuš	famɔ́za	famɔ́zaš
'all'	tódu	tóduš	tɔ́da	tɔ́daš
'ninth'	nónu	nónuš	nɔ́na	nɔ́naš
'other'	ówtru	ówtruš	ówtra	ówtraš

(b) Focus: stem alternations between low ([ɛ], [ɔ]), mid ([e], [o]), and high ([i], [u]). ("pres." = present, "ind." = indicative, "sub." = subjunctive)

	'ought'	'write'	'move'	'eat'	'sell'	'break'
pres. ind.						
1. sg.	dévu	iskrévu	móvu	kómu	vḗdu	rṍpu
2. sg.	déviš	iskréviš	móviš	kómiš	vḗdiš	rṍpiš
3. sg.	dévi	iskrévi	móvi	kómi	vḗdi	rṍpi
1. pl.	divémuš	iskrivémuš	muvémuš	kumémuš	vēdḗmuš	rõpḗmuš
3. pl.	dévẽ	iskrévẽ	móvẽ	kómẽ	vḗdẽ	rṍpẽ
pres. sub.						
1. sg.	déva	iskréva	móva	kóma	vḗda	rṍpa
2. sg.	dévaš	iskrévaš	móvaš	kómaš	vḗdaš	rṍpaš
3. sg.	déva	iskréva	móva	kóma	vḗda	rṍpa
1. pl.	divámuš	iskrivámuš	muvámuš	kumámuš	vēdámuš	rõpámuš
3. pl.	dévã	iskrévã	móvã	kómã	vḗdã	rṍpã

6. SAMOAN
Focus: variation in the formation of simple and perfective verb forms.

		simple	perfective		simple	perfective
(a)	'dwell'	nofo	nofoia	'rub'	olo	oloia
	'face'	aŋa	aŋaia	'tell'	taʔu	taʔuia
	'build'	ati	atia	'dig'	ʔeli	ʔelia
	'touch'	paʔi	paʔia	'keep'	mau	mauia
	'fly'	lele	lelea	'split'	isi	isia
	'steal'	ŋaoi	ŋaoia	'violate'	soli	solia
(b)	'stand'	tuː	tuːlia	'flow on'	au	aulia
	'think'	manatu	manatulia	'cost'	tau	taulia
	'avoid'	ʔalo	ʔalofia	'jump'	oso	osofia
	'collect'	sao	saofia	'enter'	ulu	ulufia
	'smoke'	asu	asuŋia	'question'	fesili	fesiliŋia
	'be angry'	ita	itaŋia	'bow down'	ifo	ifoŋia
	'scold'	ʔote	ʔoteŋia	'step'	laʔa	laʔasia
	'spit'	anu	anusia	'throw'	velo	velosia
	'cry'	taŋi	taŋisia	'break'	motu	motusia
	'be lodged'	api	apitia	'be raised'	eʔe	eʔetia
	'meet'	fono	fonotia	'fall (dew)'	sau	sautia
	'be able'	lavaː	lavaːtia	'arrive'	oʔo	oʔotia
	'cover up'	tanu	tanumia	'forget'	ŋalo	ŋalomia
	'admire'	moʔo	moʔomia	'want'	manaʔo	manaʔomia
	'go across'	sopo	sopoʔia	'be spoken frankly'	aːloa	aːloaʔia
	'shoot'	fana	fanaʔia			
(c)	'sing'	usu	usuina	'prop up'	teʔe	teʔeina
	'put away'	teu	teuina	'see'	iloa	iloaina
	'rain'	ua	uaina	'pinch'	uŋa	uŋaina

Unit III

7. LATIN
   Focus: variation in stems and in suffixes. ("nom." = nominative, "gen." = genitive, "abl." = ablative.)

		nom. sg.	gen. sg.	abl. sg.
(a)	'chief'	priːnkeps	priːnkipis	priːnkipe
	'city'	urps	urbis	urbe
	'leader'	duːks	duːkis	duːke
	'king'	reːks	reːgis	reːge
	'oarsman'	reːmeks	reːmigis	reːmige
	'voice'	woːks	woːkis	woːke
	'winter'	hiems	hiemis	hieme
(b)	'praise'	laws	lawdis	lawde
	'foot'	peːs	pedis	pede
	'health'	saluːs	saluːtis	saluːte
	'summer'	ajstaːs	ajstaːtis	ajstaːte
	'heir'	heːreːs	heːreːdis	heːreːde
(c)	'mountain'	moːns	montis	monte
	'death'	mors	mortis	morte
	'part'	pars	partis	parte
	'tribe'	geːns	gentis	gente
	'night'	noks	noktis	nokte
(d)	'watchman'	wigil	wigilis	wigile
	'salt'	sal	salis	sale
	'work'	labor	laboːris	laboːre
	'woman'	mulier	mulieːris	mulieːre
(e)	'lion'	leoː	leoːnis	leoːne
	'speech'	oraːtioː	oraːtioːnis	oraːtioːne
(f)	'mother'	maːter	maːtris	maːtre
	'belly'	wenter	wentris	wentre
	'father'	pater	patris	patre

CONTINUED→

(7. LATIN, CONTINUED)

(g)
'brother'	_____	fraːtris	fraːtre
'commoner'	_____	pleːbis	_____
'law'	_____	_____	leːge
'swamp'	_____	paluːdis	_____
'vagabond'	_____	erroːnis	_____
'grace'	_____	_____	dekoːre

8. ANCIENT GREEK
Focus: alternations in shape of stems and case-endings. (Pitch omitted; "nom." = nominative, "gen." = genitive, "dat." = dative.)

	nom. sg.	gen. sg.	dat. sg.	gen. pl.	dat. pl.
(a) 'salt'	hals	halos	hali	haloːn	halsi
'sheep'	ojs	ojos	oji	ojoːn	ojsi
'sow'	sys	syos	syi	syoːn	sysi
'thief'	kloːps	kloːpos	kloːpi	kloːpoːn	kloːpsi
'vein'	pʰleːps	pʰleːbos	pʰleːbi	pʰleːboːn	pʰleːpsi
'upper story'	kateːlips	kateːlipʰos	kateːlipʰi	kateːlipʰoːn	kateːlipsi
'watchman'	pʰylaks	pʰylakos	pʰylaki	pʰylakoːn	pʰylaksi
'goat'	ajks	ajgos	ajgi	ajgoːn	ajksi
'nail'	onyks	onykʰos	onykʰi	onykʰoːn	onyksi
'trumpet'	salpiŋks	salpiŋgos	salpiŋgi	salpiŋgoːn	salpiŋksi
'serf'	tʰeːs	tʰeːtos	tʰeːti	tʰeːtoːn	tʰeːsi
'grace'	kʰaris	kʰaritos	kʰariti	kʰaritoːn	kʰarisi
'hope'	elpis	elpidos	elpidi	elpidoːn	elpisi
'helmet'	korys	korytʰos	korytʰi	korytʰoːn	korysi
'nose'	riːs	riːnos	riːni	riːnoːn	riːsi
'dolphin'	delpʰiːs	delpʰiːnos	delpʰiːni	delpʰiːnoːn	delpʰiːsi
'giant'	gigaːs	gigantos	giganti	gigantoːn	gigaːsi

CONTINUED→

Unit III

(8. ANCIENT GREEK, CONTINUED)

(b) | 'beast' | tʰeːr | tʰeːros | tʰeːri | tʰeːroːn | tʰeːrsi |
| | 'nectar' | nektar | nektaros | nektari | nektaroːn | nektarsi |

(c) | 'old woman' | graws | graːos | graːi | graːoːn | grawsi |
| | 'ox, cow' | bows | boos | boi | booːn | bowsi |

(d) | 'hair' | tʰriks | trikʰos | trikʰi | trikʰoːn | tʰriksi |

(e) Extend your analysis of the above noun forms to include the following verb forms. For each verb, the first form is present, 1. sg.; the second is aorist, 1. sg.

'release'	lyːoː	elyːsa	'strike'	pajoː	epajsa
'send'	pempoː	epempsa	'write'	grapʰoː	egrapsa
'rub'	triːboː	etripsa	'press'	tʰliːboː	etʰlipsa
'weave'	plekoː	epleksa	'say'	legoː	eleksa
'bite'	brykoː	ebryksa	'cut'	koptoː	ekopsa
'choke'	pniːgoː	epniksa	'tell'	pʰrazoː	epʰrasa
'cheat'	psewdoː	epsewsa	'rot'	pyːtʰoː	epyːsa
'play'	pajzoː	epajsa	'disgrace'	eleŋkʰoː	eːleŋksa
'anticipate'	pʰtʰanoː	epʰtʰasa	'sink down'	oklazoː	oːklasa
'insult'	hybrizoː	hyːbrisa	'beg'	hiketewoː	hiːketewsa
'give to drink'	ardoː	eːrsa	'row'	eresoː	eːresa
'mark off'	horizoː	hoːrisa	'feed'	trepʰoː	etʰrepsa
'run'	trekʰoː	etʰreksa	'blame'	psegoː	epseksa
'persuade'	pejtʰoː	_____	'injure'	blaptoː	_____

(f) | 'do' | praːttoː | epraːksa | 'cook' | pettoː | epepsa |
| | 'sprinkle' | pattoː | epasa | 'dig' | oryttoː | oːryksa |

(g) Compare your solutions for these Greek data and for the Latin problem (#7).

9. RUMANIAN
Focus: variation in stems and endings.

		m. sg.	m. pl.	f. sg.	f. pl.
(a)	'rough'	áspru	áspri	ásprə	áspre
	'blue'	albástru	albáštri	albástrə	albástre
	'our'	nóstru	nóštri	no̦ástrə	no̦ástre
	'simple'	símplu	símpli	símplə	símple
(b)	'easy'	ušór	ušórʲ	ušo̦árə	ušo̦áre
	'good'	bún	búnʲ	búnə	búne
	'sad'	tríst	trííštʲ	trístə	tríste
	'kind'	amábil	amábilʲ	amábilə	amábile
	'white'	álb	álbʲ	álbə	álbe
	'new'	nów	nój	nówə	nój
(c)	'high'	ɯnált	ɯnáltsʲ	ɯnáltə	ɯnálte
	'choice'	alés	aléš	ale̦ásə	alése
	'poor'	bʲét	bʲétsʲ	bʲétə	bʲéte
	'wide'	lát	látsʲ	látə	láte
	'grand'	məréts	mərétsʲ	mərétsə	mərétse
	'haughty'	trufáš	trufáš	trufášə	trufáše
	'blond'	blónd	blónzʲ	blóndə	blónde
	'steady'	ɯntrég	ɯntréǰ	ɯntre̦ágə	---
	'hard-working'	harník	harníč	harníkə	harníče
	'beautiful'	frumós	frumóš	frumo̦ásə	frumo̦áse
	'brave'	kuražós	kuražóš	kuražo̦ásə	kuražo̦áse

Unit III

10. ZOQUE
Focus: consonant alternations in stem; allomorphs of prefix.

		noun	'my...'		noun	'my...'
(a)	'basket'	waka	nwaka	'woman'	jomo	njomo
	'cigarette'	huki	nhuki	'burro'	buřu	mbuřu
	'record'	disko	ndisko	'rooster'	gaju	ŋgaju
(b)	'clothing'	pama	mbama	'trap'	trampa	ndrampa
	'plate'	plato	mblato	'father'	tatah	ndatah
	'horse'	kaju	ŋgaju	'calabash'	t̯sima	nd̯zima
	'rabbit'	coʔŋgoja	ɲɟoʔŋgoja			
(c)	'belt'	faha	faha	'beans'	sʌk	sʌk
	'soap'	šapun	šapun	'nail'	lawus	lawus
	'corn'	mok	mok	'skin'	naka	naka

(d) Your solution should also handle the following verb forms. ("pres." = present, "imp." = imperative.)

	pres.	imp. sg.	imp. pl.
'say'	nʌmba	nʌmʌ	nʌmdamʌ
'come'	minba	minʌ	mindamʌ
'do'	cʌkpa	cʌkʌ	cʌktamʌ
'scare'	cʌknaʔt̯spa	cʌknaʔt̯sʌ	cʌknaʔt̯stamʌ

11. MWERA
Focus: alternations in shapes of li- (sg.) and ma- (pl.).

(a)	'cloud'	liunde	maunde	'hoe'	lijela	mažela
	'stone'	liganga	maganga	'hyena'	litunu	matunu
	'house-rat'	liŋgoː	maŋgoː	'hearth-stone'	liːga	maiga
(b)	'name'	liːna	mɛːna	'tooth'	liːno	mɛːno
	'eye'	liːjo	mɛːjo	'sun'	liuβa	mɔːβa

12. SPANISH (CASTILIAN)
   Focus: first, determine the placement of stress in all forms; second, compare
   groups (a) and (b), noting the stem variations in (b). Are the latter
   to be accounted for by phonological or by morphological conditioning?
   Key to forms:
   1. 1. sg. present indicative   5. gerund
   2. 2. sg. present indicative   6. 1. sg. present subjunctive
   3. 1. pl. present indicative   7. 2. sg. present subjunctive
   4. 1. sg. imperfect indicative   8. 1. pl. present subjunctive

(a)

	'change'	'hate'	'eulogize'	'reward'	'rage'	'forge'	'attest'
1	kámbjo	óðjo	elóxjo	prémjo	r̄áβjo	fráɣwo	atestíɣwo
2	kámbjas	óðjas	elóxjas	prémjas	r̄áβjas	fráɣwas	atestíɣwas
3	kambjámos	oðjámos	eloxjámos	premjámos	r̄aβjámos	fraɣwámos	atestiɣwámos
4	kambjáβa	oðjáβa	eloxjáβa	premjáβa	r̄aβjáβa	fraɣwáβa	atestiɣwáβa
5	kambjándo	oðjándo	eloxjándo	premjándo	r̄aβjándo	fraɣwándo	atestiɣwándo
6	kámbje	óðje	elóxje	prémje	r̄áβje	fráɣwe	atestíɣwe
7	kámbjes	óðjes	elóxjes	prémjes	r̄áβjes	fráɣwes	atestíɣwes
8	kambjémos	oðjémos	eloxjémos	premjémos	r̄aβjémos	fraɣwémos	atestiɣwémos

(b)

	'send'	'vary'	'watch'	'empty'	'adorn'	'ally'	'act'	'continue'
1	embío	barío	bixío	baθío	ataβío	alío	aktúo	kontinúo
2	embías	barías	bixías	baθías	ataβías	alías	aktúas	kontinúas
3	embjámos	barjámos	bixjámos	baθjámos	ataβjámos	aljámos	aktwámos	kontinwámos
4	embjáβa	barjáβa	bixjáβa	baθjáβa	ataβjáβa	aljáβa	aktwáβa	kontinwáβa
5	embjándo	barjándo	bixjándo	baθjándo	ataβjándo	aljándo	aktwándo	kontinwándo
6	embíe	baríe	bixíe	baθíe	ataβíe	alíe	aktúe	kontinúe
7	embíes	baríes	bixíes	baθíes	ataβíes	alíes	aktúes	kontinúes
8	embjémos	barjémos	bixjémos	baθjémos	ataβjémos	aljémos	aktwémos	kontinwémos

Unit III

13. SWAHILI
Focus: allomorphs of adjective stems and class prefixes.

with nouns of class...	2	7	8	9-10
(a) 'nice'	wazuri	kizuri	vizuri	nzuri
'bad'	wabaja	kibaja	vibaja	mbaja
'little'	wadogo	kidogo	vidogo	ndogo
'hard'	wagumu	kigumu	vigumu	ŋgumu
(b) 'broad'	wapana	kipana	vipana	pʰana
'sweet'	watamu	kitamu	vitamu	tʰamu
'bitter'	wačuŋgu	kičuŋgu	vičuŋgu	čʰuŋgu
'big'	wakubwa	kikubwa	vikubwa	kʰubwa
(c) 'fat'	wanono	kinono	vinono	nono
'one'	wamoǰa	kimoǰa	vimoǰa	moǰa
'jealous'	wawivu	kiwivu	viwivu	mbivu
'long'	warefu	kirefu	virefu	ndefu
(d) 'four'	wane	kine	vine	nne
'new'	wapja	kipja	vipja	mpja
'female'	wake	kike	vike	ŋke
(e) 'other'	weŋgine	kiŋgine	viŋgine	ɲiŋgine
'red'	wekundu	čekundu	vjekundu	ɲekundu
'soft'	waororo	čororo	vjororo	ɲororo
'white'	weupe	čeupe	vjeupe	ɲeupe

14. DUTCH
    Focus: formation of infinitive ("inf."), past tense, and past participle
           ("pcp."). (Accents = stress.)

	inf.	past	pcp.		inf.	past	pcp.
'cook'	kókə	kóktə	xəkókt	'build'	bɔ́wə	bɔ́wdə	xəbɔ́wt
'hear'	hórə	hórdə	xəhórt	'order'	bəstélə	bəstéldə	bəstélt
'live'	lévə	lévdə	xəléft	'talk'	práˤːtə	práˤːtə	xəpráˤːt
'travel'	rǽjzə	rǽjzdə	xərǽjst	'meet'	ɔntmútə	ɔntmútə	ɔntmút
'shake'	sxýdə	sxýdə	xəsxýt	'follow'	vólɣə	vólɣdə	xəvólxt
'hope'	hópə	hóptə	xəhópt	'play'	spélə	spéldə	xəspélt
'be OK'	sxíkə	sxíktə	xəsxíkt	'laugh'	láxə	láxtə	(xəláxə)
'cry'	hœ́ɥlə	hœ́ɥldə	xəhœ́ɥlt				

15. PAME (OTOMÍ)
    Focus: stem changes before the possessive suffixes -p ('its, his, her'),
           -bm? ('our'), -pt ('their'), and -k ('my'). (Accents = tones.)

(a)	'sandals'	nlhót͡s?	nlhóspt	'cracker'	šikjàič?	šikjàišp
	'bag'	waŋgóč	waŋgóšk	'lamp'	šikkìč?	šikkìšpt
(b)	'cloth'	šôt	šôp	'fan'	šilhèik	šilhèpt
	'skirt'	šilhôl?	šilhôlp			
(c)	'enemy'	mi?ìo	mi?ìp	'name'	ŋgolhṍ?	ŋgolhópt
	'chamales'	rómmɛo?	rómmɛbm?	'abdomen'	konhôi	konhôp
	'grandmother'	rattòi	rattòbm?	'smoke'	ski?i	ski?ep
	'trousers'	naŋkhòi?	naŋkhò?p			
(d)	'head'	kanhã̀oŋ	kanhã̀mpt	'messenger'	ŋgobái	ŋgobépt
	'song'	nimbjã̃i?	nimbjɛ̃?p / nimbjɛ̃pt			

Unit III

16. CATALAN
Focus: alternations in stems. (Accents = stress.)

		m.	f.		m.	f.
(a)	'young'	žóβə	žóβə	'wide'	ámplə	ámplə
	'that'	əkéʎ	əkéʎə	'enough'	típ	típə
	'shy'	əskérp	əskérpə	'small'	pətít	pətítə
	'drenched'	šóp	šópə	'dirty'	brút	brútə
	'dry'	sɛ́k	sɛ́kə	'little'	pɔ́k	pɔ́kə
	'thick'	əspɛ́s	əspɛ́sə	'sad'	tríst	trístə
	'low'	báš	bášə	'fat'	grás	grásə
	'lame'	kóš	kóšə			
(b)	'flat'	plá	plánə	'light'	klá	klárə
	'hard'	dú	dúrə	'distant'	ʎuɲá	ʎuɲánə
	'round'	ruðó	ruðónə	'good'	bɔ́	bɔ́nə
(c)	'blind'	órp	órβə	'mute'	mút	múðə
	'empty'	bwít	bwíðə	'cold'	frɛ́t	frɛ́ðə
	'yellow'	grók	gróɣə	'fearful'	purúk	purúɣə
	'heavy'	fəšúk	fəšúɣə	'gray'	grís	grízə
	'English'	əŋglɛ́s	əŋglɛ́zə			
(d)	'blue'	bláw	bláβə	'live'	bíw	bíβə
	'soft'	tów	tóβə			
(e)	'crazy'	bóč	bóžə	'red'	rɔ́č	rɔ́žə
	'ugly'	ʎéč	ʎéjə	'middle'	míč	míjə
(f)	'white'	bláŋ	bláŋkə	'deep'	prufún	prufúndə
	'hot'	kəlén	kəléntə	'ill'	məlá˃ɫ	məlá˃ɫtə
	'strong'	fórt	fórtə	'long'	ʎárk	ʎárɣə

(g) Compare your solution for Catalan with the one you arrive at for French (following problem); how are they similar, and how are they different?

17. FRENCH
    Focus: as in preceding Catalan problem. (r = [R]; accents = stress.)

		m.	f.		m.	f.
(a)	'dear'	šɛ́r	šɛ́rə	'better'	mɛjœ́r	mɛjœ́rə
	'none'	nýl	nýlə	'mortal'	mɔrtɛ́l	mɔrtɛ́lə
	'public'	pyblík	pyblíkə	'Greek'	grɛ́k	grɛ́kə
(b)	'brave'	kuražǿ	kuražǿzə	'deep'	prɔfɔ̃́	prɔfɔ̃́də
	'ugly'	lɛ́	lɛ́də	'green'	vɛ́r	vɛ́rtə
	'white'	blɑ̃́	blɑ̃́šə	'small'	pətí	pətítə
	'short'	kúr	kúrtə	'thick'	epɛ́	epɛ́sə
	'envious'	žalú	žalúzə	'slow'	lɑ̃́	lɑ̃́tə
	'sweet'	dú	dúsə	'high'	ó	ótə
	'low'	bá	básə	'long'	lɔ̃́	lɔ̃́gə
	'favorite'	favorí	favorítə	'exempt'	frɑ̃́	frɑ̃́šə
	'big'	grɑ̃́	grɑ̃́də	'nice'	žãtí	žãtíɟə
	'cool'	frɛ́	frɛ́šə	'blessed'	bení	benítə
(c)	'short'	brɛ́f	brɛ́və	'active'	aktíf	aktívə
(d)	'fine'	fɛ̃́	fínə	'good'	bɔ̃́	bɔ́nə
	'next'	prɔšɛ̃́	prɔšɛ́nə	'malicious'	malɛ̃́	malíɲə
	'brown'	brœ̃́	brýnə	'peasant'	pɛjzɑ̃́	pɛjzánə
(e)	'stupid'	só	sótə	'fat'	gró	grósə or groĩs
	'uneasy'	ɛ̃kjé	ɛ̃kjɛ́tə	'first'	prəmjé	prəmjɛ́rə
	'light'	ležé	ležɛ́rə	'complete'	kɔ̃plé	kɔ̃plɛ́tə
(f)	'blue'	blǿ	blǿ	'old'	ažé	ažé
	'sharp'	ɛgý	ɛgý	'pretty'	žɔlí	žɔlí
	'young'	žœ́nə	žœ́nə	'red'	rúžə	rúžə

(g) Write a rule governing the placement of stress in French.
(h) In modern colloquial French, final [ə] has dropped. Assume that the schwa is missing in the above data; how does this affect your analysis?

Unit III

18. MAGYAR (HUNGARIAN)
Focus: formation of plural, and resultant changes in stems. (Note: for the purposes of your solution, you may consider geminate vowels as single long vowels, or as distinct segments.)

		sg.	pl.		sg.	pl.
(a)	'muscle'	izom	izmok	'hook'	horog	horgok
	'lair'	vɒtsok	vɒtskok	'petal'	sirom	sirmok
	'lute'	koboz	kobzok	'curse'	aatok	aatkok
	'owl'	bɒgoj	bɒgjok	'sheepfold'	ɒkol	ɒklok
	'wrapper'	burok	burkok	'tower'	toroɲ	torɲok
(b)	'grove'	berek	berkek	'strawberry'	eper	eprek
	'worm'	feereg	feergek	'cover'	lepel	leplek
	'twin'	iker	ikrek	'saddle'	ɲereg	ɲergek
	'hayrick'	kɒzɒl	kɒzlɒk	'lip'	ɒjɒk	ɒjkɒk
	'vat'	čøbør	čøbrøk	'horn'	tyløk	tylkøk
	'knot'	bycøk	byckøk	'bucket'	vødør	vødrøk
(c)	'gut'	beel	belek	'mouse'	egeer	egerek
	'root'	jøkeer	jøkerek	'sparrow'	vereeb	verebek
	'chalk'	mees	mesek	'cow'	texeen	texenek
(d)	'sir'	uur	urɒk	'pole'	ruud	rudɒk
	'bridge'	hiid	hidɒk	'tendon'	iin	inɒk
	'horse'	loo	lovok	'word'	soo	sook
	'crane'	dɒru	dɒrvɒk	'gravy'	lee	levek
	'louse'	tety	tetvek	'maggot'	ɲyy	ɲyvek
	'ash'	hɒmu	hɒmvɒk			
(e)	'insect'	bogaar	bogɒrɒk	'ray'	šugaar	šugɒrɒk
	'swamp'	močaar	močɒrɒk	'bird'	mɒdaar	mɒdɒrɒk

(f) Is rounding distinctive for low vowels?

19. DYIRBAL
    Focus: variation in case endings

	(a) nominative	ergative	locative	(b) genitive
'rainbow'	jamani	jamanigu	jamaniga	jamaniŋu
'snake'	wadam	wadambu	wadamba	wadamu
'possum'	midin	midindu	midinda	midinu
'small lizard'	biɲɉiriɲ	biɲɉiriɲɉu	biɲɉiriɲɉa	biɲɉiriɲu
'brown snake'	walguj	walgujɉu	walgujɉa	walgujŋu
'woman'	ɉugumbil	ɉugumbiṛu	ɉugumbiṛa	ɉugumbilŋu
'bee'	gubur	guburu	gubuṛa	guburŋu
'black guano'	gugaṛ	gugaṛu	gugaṛa	gugaṛŋu

20. MARGI
    Focus: tone alternations in person-number endings.

(a)

		...run'		...drink'		...sit'		...can take'		...walk'
'I		jú		jú		jú		jú		jú
'you (sg.)		gù		gù		gù		gù		gù
'he		ɉá		ɉà		ɉá		ɉà		ɉá
'we both	wì	má	àsá	mà	índà	má	àxər	mà	áβə̀	má
'we (excl.)		ʔjá		ʔjà		ʔjá		ʔjà		ʔjá
'we (incl.)		mə́r		mə̀r		mə́r		mə̀r		mə́r
'you (pl.)		ɲí		ɲì		ɲí		ɲì		ɲí
'they		ndá		ndà		ndá		ndà		ndá

(b) Supply the tones of the person-number markers for the following verbs.

| 'let rot' | ìdáná | 'be a Higi' | hə̀ɉì |
| 'work' | àʔíɬə̀r | 'be a Margi' | màrɉí |

Unit III   87

21. GERMAN
    Focus: placement of stress in verbs whose prefixes (underlined) separate
           and permute in the present tense, and those whose prefixes do not.
           Internal morphological structure is important here. (r = [ʀ])

(a)   <u>infinitive</u>   <u>present</u>   <u>infinitive & present</u>

   'depart'   <u>ʔáp</u>fàːrən   fàːrən <u>ʔáp</u>   'perpetrate'   fɛr<u>ʔýːbən</u>

   'put on'   <u>ʔán</u>tsìːən   tsìːən <u>ʔán</u>   'describe'   bə<u>šrájbən</u>

   'ascribe'   <u>tsúː</u>šràjbən   šràjbən <u>tsúː</u>   'cut to pieces'   <u>tsɛršnájdən</u>

   'provide'   <u>fór</u>zèːən   zèːən <u>fór</u>   'seize'   ʔɛr<u>grájfən</u>

   'direct'   <u>ʔán</u>ʔɔ̀rdnən   ʔɔ̀rdnən <u>ʔán</u>   'escape'   ʔɛnt<u>kómən</u>

   'perish'   <u>ʔúntər</u>gèːən   gèːən <u>ʔúntər</u>   'occupy'   bə<u>vóːnən</u>

   'transform'   <u>ʔúːm</u>ʔɛ̀ndərn   ʔɛ̀ndərn <u>ʔúːm</u>   'revere'   fɛr<u>ʔéːrən</u>

   'dedicate'   <u>tsúː</u>ʔàjgnən   ʔàjgnən <u>tsúː</u>   'publish'   fɛr<u>ʔǿfəntlɪçən</u>

   'get back'   <u>víːdər</u>hòːlən   hòːlən <u>víːdər</u>   'repeat'   vìːdər<u>hóːlən</u>

   'drive around'   <u>ʔúːm</u>fàːrən   fàːrən <u>ʔúːm</u>   'avoid'   ʔùːm<u>fáːrən</u>

   'break through'   <u>dúrç</u>brɛ̀çən   brɛ̀çən <u>dúrç</u>   'pierce'   dùrç<u>bréçən</u>

(b) Is [ʔ] distinctive, or can its distribution be predicted by rule?

22. SPANISH (CASTILIAN)
    Focus: placement of stress in derived forms. Key to suffixes: -<u>eθ</u> and -<u>iðað</u>
           = noun derived from adjective ('-ness,' '-ity'); -<u>isimo</u> = 'very';
           -<u>mente</u> = adverb derived from adjective ('-ly'). Again, internal
           structure is important here, especially for (b).

(a) 'easy'   fáθil   faθiliðáð   faθilísimo   (b) fáθilmènte

    'haughty'   altíβo   altiβéθ   altiβísimo   altíβamènte

    'versatile'   bɛrsátil   bɛrsatiliðáð   bɛrsatilísimo   bɛrsátilmènte

    'neat'   nítiðo   nitiðéθ   nitiðísimo   nítiðamènte

    'famous'   θéleβre   θeleβriðáð   θeleβrísimo   θéleβremènte

    'happy'   felíθ   feliθiðáð   feliθísimo   felíθmènte

    'next'   próksimo   proksimiðáð   proksimísimo   próksimamènte

    'fast'   r̄ápiðo   r̄apiðéθ   r̄apiðísimo   r̄ápiðamènte

    'simple'   senθíʎo   senθiʎéθ   senθiʎísimo   senθíʎamènte

23. FULA
Focus: formation of causative. (In the continuous tense forms, -o and -a
= middle and active voice, respectively; this is irrelevant here.)

		continuous	causative		continuous	causative
(a)	'come out'	wurto	wurtina	'arrive'	jotto	jottina
	'steal'	wujja	wujjina	'get down'	ǰippo	ǰippina
	'be deep'	lugga	luggina	'rise up'	ʔummo	ʔummina
(b)	'fear'	hula	hulna	'laugh'	ǰala	ǰalna
	'drink'	jara	jarna	'be a Moslem'	ǰuːla	ǰuːlna
	'cry'	woja	wojna	'stop'	daro	darna
(c)	'be bitter'	ɲaːɗa	ɲaɗɗina	'be chief'	laːmo	lammina
	'be full'	heːwa	hebbina	'be long'	ǰuːta	ǰuttina
	'pull up'	ɗoːfa	ɗoppina	'be wide'	jaːǰa	jaǰǰina
	'go to sleep'	ɗaːno	ɗannina	'forgive'	jaːfa	jappina

24. LOGBARA
Focus: variation in vowels and final consonants of stems. (Tone omitted.)

		'my'	'his'	'our'	'your (sg.)'	'your (pl.)'	'their'
(a)	'goats'	diegi	diegina	dieginɛ	diegiwa	diegini	diegiwu	diegigï
	'man'	daːno	daːnona	daːnonɛ	daːnowa	dɐːnoni	dɐːnowu	daːnogï
	'head of game'	leː	leːna	leːnɛ	leːwa	leːni	leːwu	leːgï
(b)	'snake'	twoːl	twoːla	twoːlɛ	twoːlwa	twoːli	twoːlwu	twoːlgï
	'chair'	kɔːm	kɔːma	kɔːmɛ	kɔːmwa	koːmi	koːmwu	kɔːmgï
	'cow'	djaːŋ	djaːŋa	djaːŋɛ	djaːŋwa	djɐːŋi	djɐːŋwu	djaːŋgï
	'goat'	djɛːl	djɛːla	djɛːlɛ	djɛːlwa	djeːli	djeːlwu	djɛːlgï
	'body'	kʊːm	kʊːma	kʊːmɛ	kʊːmwa	kuːmi	kuːmwu	kʊːmgï
	'nose'	uːm	uːma	uːmɛ	uːmwa	uːmi	uːmwu	uːmgï
	'tree'	jaːt	jaːta	jaːtɛ	jaːtwa	jɐːti	jɐːtwu	jaːtgï
(c)	'daughter'	ɲaː	ɲaːra	ɲaːrɛ	ɲaːwa	ɲɐːri	ɲɐːwu	ɲaːgï
	'hair'	jeː	jeːra	jeːrɛ	jeːwa	jeːri	jeːwu	jeːgï

Unit III

25. KIKUYU
Focus: alternations in prefixes and suffixes in (a-e); your analysis should be general enough to account likewise for (f-g), a different formation. (Tone omitted.)

		simple	perfect		simple	perfect
(a)	'strangle'	ita	ňǰiteetɛ	'come'	oka	ňǰokeetɛ
	'miss'	aɣa	ňǰaɣeetɛ	'get out of the way'	ɛhɛra	ňǰɛhɛrɛɛtɛ
(b)	'lop off'	βura	mbureetɛ	'churn'	βɔča	mbɔčɛɛtɛ
	'cut'	tɛma	ndɛmɛɛtɛ	'send'	toma	ndomeetɛ
	'pay'	reha	ndeheetɛ	'jump'	rooɣa	ndooɣeetɛ
	'cross'	kera	ŋgereetɛ	'carry'	kuua	ŋguueetɛ
	'reap'	ɣɛða	ŋgɛðɛɛtɛ	'burn'	čina	ňǰineetɛ
	'sleep'	kɔma	ŋgɔmɛɛtɛ	'buy'	ɣora	ŋgoreetɛ
(c)	'cultivate'	rema	nemeetɛ	'disobey'	rɛma	nɛmɛɛtɛ
	'strike'	riiŋga	niiŋgeetɛ	'tell'	ɣana	ŋaneetɛ
(d)	'know'	mɛɲa	mɛɲɛɛtɛ	'catch'	ɲiita	ɲiiteetɛ
	'finish'	niina	niineetɛ	'snore'	ŋɔrɔta	ŋɔrɔtɛɛtɛ
(e)	'come up'	ambata	ɲambateetɛ	'write'	andeka	ɲandekeetɛ
	'separate'	amora	ɲamoreetɛ	'see'	ɔna	ɲɔnɛɛtɛ

		sg.	pl.		sg.	pl.
(f)	'rib'	roβaru	mbaru	'seam'	rotumɔ	ndumɔ
	'tongue'	roreme	neme	'tail hair'	rokɔrɛ	ŋgɔrɛ
	'piece of wood'	roko	ŋgo	'backbone'	ročuðe	ňǰuðe
	'fence'	roɣiri	ŋgiri			
(g)	'story'	roɣana	ŋana	'blade of grass'	roɲɛki	ɲɛki
	'river'	rooe	ňǰoe			

26. FRENCH

Focus: stem alternations. Key to forms: <u>1</u> = 1, 2, 3 sg. present; <u>2</u> = 1 pl. present; <u>3</u> = 2 pl. present; <u>4</u> = 3 pl. present; <u>5</u> = 1, 2, 3 sg. imperfect. (<u>r</u> = [ʀ]; accents = stress.)

(a)

	'read'	'lead'	'put'	'beat'	'leave'	'feel'	'break'	'grind'	'know'	'end'
1	lí	kɔ̃dɥí	mé	bá	pár	sã́	rɔ̃́	mú	kɔné	finí
2	lizɔ̃́	kɔ̃dɥizɔ̃́	mɛtɔ̃́	batɔ̃́	partɔ̃́	sãtɔ̃́	rɔ̃pɔ̃́	mulɔ̃́	kɔnɛsɔ̃́	finisɔ̃́
3	lizé	kɔ̃dɥizé	mɛté	baté	parté	sãté	rɔ̃pé	mulé	kɔnɛsé	finisé
4	lízə	kɔ̃dɥízə	métə	bátə	pártə	sã́tə	rɔ̃́pə	múlə	kɔnɛ́sə	finísə
5	lizɛ́	kɔ̃kɥizɛ́	mɛtɛ́	batɛ́	partɛ́	sãtɛ́	rɔ̃pɛ́	mulɛ́	kɔnɛsɛ́	finisɛ́

	'grow'	'believe'	'flee'	'boil'	'live'	'serve'	'sleep'	'defeat'	'run'	'conclude'
1	krwá	krwá	fɥí	bú	ví	sɛ́r	dɔ́r	vɛ̃́	kúr	kɔ̃klý
2	krwasɔ̃́	krwajɔ̃́	fɥijɔ̃́	bujɔ̃́	vivɔ̃́	sɛrvɔ̃́	dɔrmɔ̃́	vɛ̃kɔ̃́	kurɔ̃́	kɔ̃klɥɔ̃́
3	krwasé	krwajé	fɥijé	bujé	vivé	sɛrvé	dɔrmé	vɛ̃ké	kuré	kɔ̃klɥé
4	krwásə	krwájə	fɥíjə	bújə	vívə	sɛ́rvə	dɔ́rmə	vɛ̃́kə	kúrə	kɔ̃klýə
5	krwasɛ́	krwajɛ́	fɥijɛ́	bujɛ́	vivɛ́	sɛrvɛ́	dɔrmɛ́	vɛ̃kɛ́	kurɛ́	kɔ̃klɥɛ́

	'follow'	'sew'	(b)	'paint'	'fear'	'take'	'come'	'hold'
1	_____	_____		pɛ̃́	krɛ̃́	prã́	vjɛ̃́	tjɛ̃́
2	_____	_____		pɛɲɔ̃́	krɛɲɔ̃́	prənɔ̃́	vənɔ̃́	tənɔ̃́
3	sɥivé	kuzé		pɛɲé	krɛɲé	prəné	vəné	təné
4	_____	_____		pɛ́ɲə	krɛ́ɲə	prénə	vjénə	tjénə
5	_____	_____		pɛɲɛ́	krɛɲɛ́	prənɛ́	vənɛ́	tənɛ́

(c)

	'drink'	'receive'	'know'	'can'	'die'	'want'	'be worth'	'resolve'
1	bwá	rəswá	sé	pǿ	mœ́r	vǿ	vó	rezý
2	byvɔ̃́	rəsəvɔ̃́	savɔ̃́	puvɔ̃́	murɔ̃́	vulɔ̃́	valɔ̃́	rezɔlvɔ̃́
3	byvé	rəsəvé	savé	puvé	muré	vulé	valé	rezɔlvé
4	bwávə	rəswávə	sávə	pǿvə	mǿvə	vǿlə	válə	rezɔ́lvə
5	byvɛ́	rəsəvɛ́	savɛ́	puvɛ́	muvɛ́	vulɛ́	valɛ́	rezɔlvɛ́

Unit III

27. KANURI
Focus: the suffix -ma ('-er, seller of ..., person associated with ...'), the tone it acquires, and tonal changes it induces in the stem. (Note: Kanuri distinguishes front [a‹] from back [a›].)

(a)
'trade'	fá‹tké	fá‹tkémà›	'bucket'	kə́rβí	kə́rβímà›
'drum'	kóló	kólómà›	'anvil'	ká›gə́l	ká›ə́lmà›
'fiddle'	kúgú	kúgúmà›	'fable'	kà›rá›βú	kà›rá›βúmà›
'basket'	zògó	zògómà›	'message'	kà›tùnó	kà›tùnómà›
'shoe'	súnó	súnómà›	'mat'	lá‹gə̀rà›	lá‹gə̀rà›mà
'hunt'	bà›rà›	bà›rà›mà›			

(b)
'pot'	bá‹zà‹m	bà‹zà‹mmá›	'food'	bə́rì	bə̀rìmá›
'complaint'	búrgù	bùrgùmá›	'work'	čídà›	čìdà›má›
'book'	kìtá›βù	kìtà›βumá›	'honey'	kəmá›gèn	kəmà›gə̀nmá›
'wind'	kǎ›rwà›	kà›rwà›má›	'milk'	čâ›m	čà›mmá›
'pot'	ňjê	ňjèmá›	'fever'	kà›ŋgê	kà›ŋgèmá›
'load'	kà›tkûn	kà›tkùnmá›			

28. MOHAVE
Focus: alternations of forms between two sets of numerals. Note that '4' and '6' seem irregular, and may require special treatment if both sets are to be derived from one.

	Set A	Set B		Set A	Set B
'1'	seto	hate:s	'6'	si:nt	ti:vs
'2'	havi:k	haki:v	'7'	vi:k	kiv
'3'	hamo:k	hako:m	'8'	mu:k	ku:m
'4'	čumpa:p	čumka:p	'9'	pa:j	aja:v
'5'	θara:p	θapa:r	'10'	ara:p	apa:r

29. TAMAZIGHT (BERBER)

Focus: consonant alternations in the two forms shown. Determine first of all how the intensive is formed, using the data in (a). Next, determine an underlying representation for the consonantism in (b) which will facilitate the derivation of both forms. (Note: geminates might also be interpreted as long or fortis consonants.)

		zero form	intensive		zero form	intensive
(a)	'spread'	əfsər	fəssər	'be extinguished'	əxsəj	xəssəj
	'cover'	əɣməs	ɣəmməs	'build'	əβnu	βənnu
	'dip'	ərfəs	rəffəs	'scratch'	əçməz	çəmməz
	'sew'	əɟnu	ɟənnu	'tear'	efləj	fəlləj
	'saw'	ənžər	nəžžər	'scratch'	ənšəf	nəššəf
	'open'	ərzəm	rəzzəm	'rub'	əmrəj	mərrəj
(b)	'be nosy'	ənβəš	nəbbəš	'roll couscous'	əfθəl	fəttəl
	'start'	əβðu	βəddu	'harvest'	əmɟər	məggər
	'kill'	nəɣ	nəqqa	'kick'	ərçəl	rəkkəl
	'ramble'	ərβəl	rəbbəl	'hide'	ənθəl	nəttəl
	'insult'	ərɟəm	rəggəm	'become buttermilk'	ənðu	nədda
	'be warm'	rəɣ	rəqqa	'boil'	ərçəm	rəkkəm
(c)	'go out'	əffəɣ	ttəffəɣ	'take off'	əkkəs	ttəkkəs
	'lock'	əqqən	ttəqqən			

30. OLD HIGH GERMAN

Focus: variation in stem vowels

	'I'	'you (sg.)'	'he'	'we'	'you (pl.)'	'they'
'wash'	wasku	waskis	waskit	waskeme:s	wasket	waskant
'tie'	bintu	bintis	bintit	binteme:s	bintet	bintant
'take'	nimu	nimis	nimit	nɛmeme:s	nɛmet	nɛmant
'lie'	liugu	liugis	liugit	liogeme:s	lioget	liogant
'speak'	sprixu	sprixis	sprixit	sprɛxeme:s	sprɛxet	sprɛxant
'offer'	biutu	biutis	biutit	bioteme:s	biotet	biotant
'weave'	wibu	wibis	wibit	wɛbeme:s	wɛbet	wɛbant

Unit III

31. OLD NORSE
    Focus: vowel alternations. ("inf." = infinitive; "imp." = imperative.)

	inf.	1. sg.	3. sg.	1. pl.	3. pl.	2. sg. imp.	2. pl. imp.
'dig'	grava	grɛv	grɛvr	grɔvum	grava	grav	gravið
'give'	geva	gev	gevr	gevum	geva	gev	gevið
'come'	koma	køm	kømr	komum	koma	kom	komið
'bite'	biːta	biːt	biːtr	biːtum	biːta	biːt	biːtið
'pay'	gjalda	geld	geldr	gjɔldum	gjalda	gjald	gjaldið
'lie'	ljuːga	lyːg	lyːgr	ljuːgum	ljuːga	ljuːg	ljuːgið

32. RUSSIAN
    Focus: first, stem alternations in (a); second, stress shift in (b) and (c) and accompanying vowel alternations. ("nom." = nominative; "gen." = genitive.)

		nom. sg.	gen. sg.		nom. sg.	gen. sg.
(a)	'labor'	trút	trúdə	'ditch'	róf	róvə
	'snow'	snʲék	snʲégə	'tooth'	zúp	zúbə
	'enemy'	vrák	vragə	'blood'	krófʲ	krovʲə
	'garage'	garáš	garážə	'voice'	góləs	góləsə
	'moss'	móx	móxə	'taste'	fkús	fkúsə
	'guest'	gósʲtʲ	gósʲtʲə	'lesson'	urók	urókə
	'belly'	živót	živótə	'collective farm'	kalxós	kalxózə
	'factory'	zavót	zavódə	'museum'	muzʲéj	muzʲéjə
(b)	'table'	stól	stalá	'rain'	dóštʲ	daždʲá
	'pencil'	kərandáš	kərəndašá	'dictionary'	slavárʲ	sləvarʲá
(c)	'kerchief'	platók	platká	'father'	atʲéts	attsá
	'bell'	zvanók	zvanká	'day'	dʲénʲ	dʲnʲá
	'mouth'	rót	rtá	'end'	kanʲéts	kantsá
	'rug'	kavʲór	kavrá	'forehead'	lóp	lbá
	'ceiling'	pətalók	pətalká	'corner'	úgəl	uglá
	'shoe'	batʲínək	batʲínkə	'gift'	pədárək	pədárkə

33. ZULU
   Focus: formation of the diminutive (second form given), and accompanying stem changes. (Tone omitted; accents = stress.)

(a) 'slice'   uːɺéːzu   ùːɺezu̯áːna   'fowl'   iŋk'úːku   ìŋk'uku̯áːna

    'food'   ukúːɓa   ùkuɓáːna   'goat'   ìmbúːzi   ìmbuzáːna

    'stone'   íːč'ɛ   iːč'áːna   'thing'   íːnt'ɔ   int'ɔáːna

    'person'   umúːnt'u   ùmunt'u̯áːna   'cloud'   íːfu   iːfu̯áːna

(b) 'feather' uːpʰáːpʰɛ   ùːpʰašáːna   'meal'   imp'úːpʰu   ìmp'ušáːna

    'meal-   uːɕúːbu   ùːɕuǰáːna   'calabash₁' ìsigúːbu   ìsiguǰáːna
     water'

    'navel'   iŋk'áːɓa   ⎫   'hill'   int'áːɓa   ìnt'ač'áːna
                          ⎬ iŋk'ač'áːna
    'ox'   iŋk'áːɓi   ⎭   'beast'   iŋk'ɔ́ːmɔ   iŋk'ɔňáːna

    'quail'   ints'u̯éːmp'a ints'u̯uňč'áːna

(c) 'time'   ìsikʰáːtʰi   ìsikʰašáːna   'book'   iȷ̃u̯áːdi   ìȷ̃u̯aǰáːna

    'egg'   iːɕáːnda   iːɕaňǰáːna   'cat'   iːk'áːt'i   ìːk'ač'áːna

    'spear'   umkʰɔ́ːnt'ɔ   ùmkʰɔňč'ɔáːna   'crowd'   ìsibukúːtʰu   ìsìbukušu̯áːna

    'bird'   iňóːni   ìňoňáːna   'dog'   íːňǰa   iňǰáːna

(d) 'calf'   iːtʰɔ́ːlɛ   iːtʰɔɓáːna   'calabash₂' ìsiɬáːli   ìsiɬaɓáːna

    'chair'   ìsiɬáːlɔ   ìsiɬaɓɔáːna   'breasts' àmaβéːlɛ   àmaβɛɓáːna

(e) 'sharp in- ùːɺʰušɛ́ːla _____   'bulge'   iːɕʰúːɓu   _____
     strument'

(f) Write a rule for stress placement in Zulu.

(g) Is vowel length always distinctive? Where is it predictable?

Unit III

34. TURKISH
Focus: first, vowel alternations in suffixes and their underlying representations; second, consonant alternations in stems and suffixes.

(a)

	absolute	accusative	dative	locative	absolute, pl.
'grape'	yzym	yzymy	yzyme	yzymde	yzymler
'end'	son	sonu	sona	sonda	sonlar
'evening'	akšam	akšamɯ	akšama	akšamda	akšamlar
'hand'	el	eli	ele	elde	eller
'name'	ad	adɯ	ada	adda	adlar
'village'	køj	køjy	køje	køjde	køjler
'totality'	kyl	kylly	kylle	kylde	kyller
'bird'	kuš	kušu	kuša	kušta	kušlar
'tree'	aač	aaǰɯ	aaǰa	aačta	aačlar
'son-in-law'	damat	damadɯ	damada	damatta	damatlar
'bottom'	dip	dibi	dibe	dipte	dipler
'horse'	at	adɯ	ada	atta	atlar
'limit'	had	haddɯ	hadda	hadda	hadlar
'crown'	tač	taǰɯ	taǰa	tačta	tačlar
'group'	grup	grubu	gruba	grupta	gruplar
'color'	renk	rengi	renge	renkte	renkler
'class'	sɯnɯf	sɯnɯffɯ	sɯnɯffa	sɯnɯfta	sɯnɯflar
'line'	hat	hattɯ	hatta	hatta	hatlar
'girl'	kɯz	kɯzɯ	kɯza	kɯzda	kɯzlar

(b) Extend your analysis to account for the following.

	absolute	'your'	'your...+pl.'
'candle'	mum	mumun	mumlarɯn
'grape'	yzym	yzymyn	yzymlerin
'lesson'	ders	dersin	derslerin
'hand'	el	elin	ellerin
'arrow'	ok	okun	oklarɯn

CONTINUED→

(34. TURKISH, CONTINUED)

(c) Extend your analysis further as a constraint on the vowel sequences in the following:

'noise'	gyrylty	'goddess'	tanrɯča
'city'	šehir	'eagle'	tavšanǰɯ
'slave'	køle	'moribund'	ølymǰyl
'his wife'	karɯsɯ		

(d) Focus: alternation of [č] and [ǰ]; underlying representation of '-ist'.

'free'	beleš	'moocher'	belešči
'work'	iš	'worker'	išči
'milk'	šyt	'milkman'	šytčy
'people'	halk	'populist'	halkčɯ
'road'	jol	'traveler'	jolǰu
'lie'	jalan	'liar'	jalanǰɯ
'zero'	sɯfɯr	'school-teacher'	sɯfɯrǰɯ
'joke'	šaka	'joker'	šakaǰɯ
'old'	eski	'old-clothes man'	_____

(e) There is another suffix (illustrated below) which alternates in the same way. Fill in the missing forms.

'white'	ak	'faded'	akčɯl
'house'	ev	'domesticated'	evǰil
'book'	kitap	'bookish'	_____
'death'	ølym	'moribund'	ølymǰyl
'fish'	balɯk	'heron'	_____
'I'	ben	'selfish'	_____
'mother'	ana	'mother's child'	_____

Unit III

35. JAPANESE

Focus: first, consonant alternations in the verb stems (see also Problem II-37); second, note that the verbs in (a) and (b) have slightly different formations; are these differences phonologically or morphologically conditioned? (Accent omitted.)

		present	nominal	gerund	past	imperative	negative
(a)	'ask'	kikɯ	kiki	kiite	kiita	kike	kikanai
	'arrive'	tsɯkɯ	tsɯki	tsɯite	tsɯita	tsɯke	tsɯkanai
	'burn'	jakɯ	jaki	jaite	jaita	jake	jakanai
	'move'	ɯŋokɯ	ɯŋoki	ɯŋoite	ɯŋoita	ɯŋoke	ɯŋokanai
	'swim'	ojoŋɯ	ojoŋi	ojoide	ojoida	ojoŋe	ojoŋanai
	'call'	jobɯ	jobi	jonde	jonda	jobe	jobanai
	'line up'	narabɯ	narabi	narande	naranda	narabe	narabanai
	'read'	jomɯ	jomi	jonde	jonda	jome	jomanai
	'relax'	jasɯmɯ	jasɯmi	jasɯnde	jasɯnda	jasɯme	jasɯmanai
	'die'	šinɯ	šini	šinde	šinda	šine	šinanai
	'ride'	norɯ	nori	notte	notta	nore	noranai
	'fall'	ɸɯrɯ	ɸɯri	ɸɯtte	ɸɯtta	ɸɯre	ɸɯranai
	'depart'	tatsɯ	tači	tatte	tatta	tate	tatanai
	'hold'	motsɯ	moči	motte	motta	mote	motanai
	'put out'	dasɯ	daši	dašite	dašita	dase	dasanai
	'dry'	hosɯ	hoši	hošite	hošita	hose	hosanai
	'pay'	haraɯ	harai	haratte	haratta	harae	harawanai
	'differ'	čiŋaɯ	čiŋai	čiŋatte	čiŋatta	čiŋae	čiŋawanai
	'employ'	jatoɯ	jatoi	jatotte	jatotta	jatoe	jatowanai
(b)	'eat'	taberɯ	tabe	tabete	tabeta	tabero	tabenai
	'insert'	irerɯ	ire	irete	ireta	irero	irenai
	'descend'	orirɯ	ori	orite	orita	oriro	orinai
(c)	'change'	kaerɯ	_____	_____	_____	_____	kaenai
	'return'	kaerɯ	_____	_____	_____	_____	kaeranai

36. ITALIAN

Focus: first, vowel alternations in stems; second, consonant alternations in (c). ("pres." = present; "imperf." = imperfect; "ind." = indicative; "sub." = subjunctive. Accents = stress.)

		pres. ind. 1. sg.	2. sg.	3. sg.	1. pl.	3. pl.	pres. sub. 1. sg.	imperf. ind. 1. sg.
(a)	'drink'	bévo	bévi	béve	bevjámo	bévono	béva	bevévo
	'put'	métto	métti	métte	mettjámo	méttono	métta	mettévo
	'write'	skrívo	skrívi	skríve	skrivjámo	skrívono	skríva	skrivévo
	'break'	rómpo	rómpi	rómpe	rompjámo	rómpono	rómpa	rompévo
	'sell'	véndo	véndi	vénde	vendjámo	véndono	vénda	vendévo
(b)	'ask'	kjɛ́do	kjɛ́di	kjɛ́de	kjedjámo	kjɛ́dono	kjɛ́da	kjedévo
	'take'	prɛ́ndo	prɛ́ndi	prɛ́nde	prendjámo	prɛ́ndono	prɛ́nda	prendévo
	'sit down'	sjɛ́do	sjɛ́di	sjɛ́de	sedjámo	sjɛ́dono	sjɛ́da	sedévo
	'cook'	kwɔ́čo	kwɔ́či	kwɔ́če	kočámo	kwɔ́čono	kwɔ́ča	kočévo
	'move'	mwɔ́vo	mwɔ́vi	mwɔ́ve	movjámo	mwɔ́vono	mwɔ́va	movévo
	'lose'	pɛ́rdo	pɛ́rdi	pɛ́rde	perdjámo	pɛ́rdono	pɛ́rda	perdévo
	'shake'	skwɔ́to	skwɔ́ti	skwɔ́te	skotjámo	skwɔ́tono	skwɔ́ta	skotévo
(c)	'root out'	svɛ́lgo	svɛ́ʎi	svɛ́ʎe	sveʎámo	svɛ́lgono	svɛ́lga	sveʎévo
	'take away'	tólgo	tóʎi	tóʎe	toʎámo	tólgono	tólga	toʎévo
	'select'	šélgo	šéʎi	šéʎe	šeʎámo	šélgono	šélga	šeʎévo
	'win'	vínko	vínči	vínče	vinčámo	vínkono	vínka	vinčévo
	'twist'	tórko	tórči	tórče	torčámo	tórkono	tórka	torčévo
	'say'	díko	díči	díče	dičámo	díkono	díka	dičévo
	'cash'	ezígo	ezíǰi	ezíǰe	eziǰámo	ezígono	ezíga	eziǰévo
	'break'	frángo	fránǰi	fránǰe	franǰámo	frángono	fránga	franǰévo
	'know'	konósko	konóši	konóše	konošámo	konóskono	konóska	konošévo
	'pour'	mésko	méši	méše	mešámo	méskono	méska	mešévo

(d) How is the solution to vowel alternation in Italian verbs similar to that in Spanish verbs (Introduction, <u>To the Student</u>, Sample Problem 2). How does it differ?

Unit III

37. RUSSIAN
Focus: stems and endings; ignore (for now) stress shifts and vowel changes.

		infinitive	1. sg.	2. sg.	3. pl.
(a)	'praise'	xəvalʲítʲ	xəvalʲú	xaválʲiš	xaválʲət
	'speak'	gəvarʲítʲ	gəvarʲú	gəvarʲíš	gəvarʲát
	'execute'	kaznʲítʲ	kaznʲú	káznʲiš	káznʲət
	'remember'	pómnʲitʲ	pómnʲu	pómnʲiš	pómnʲət
	'smoke'	kurʲítʲ	kurʲú	kúrʲiš	kúrʲət
	'wound'	ránʲitʲ	ránʲu	ránʲiš	ránʲət
	'decide'	rʲišítʲ	rʲišú	rʲišíš	rʲišát
	'end'	kónčitʲ	kónču	kónčiš	kónčət
	'lay down'	pəlažítʲ	pəlažú	palóžiš	palóžət
	'hold'	dʲiržítʲ	dʲiržú	dʲéržiš	dʲéržət
	'be employed'	spužítʲ	spužú	spúžiš	spúžət
(b)	'load'	gruzʲítʲ	gružú	grúzʲiš	grúzʲət
	'carry'	nasʲítʲ	našú	nósʲiš	nósʲət
	'shine'	svʲitʲítʲ	svʲiču	svʲétʲiš	svʲétʲət
	'joke'	šutʲítʲ	šuču	šútʲiš	šútʲət
	'pay'	platʲítʲ	plaču	platʲíš	platʲát
	'go'	xadʲítʲ	xažú	xódʲiš	xódʲət
	'clean'	čísʲtʲitʲ	číšču	čísʲtʲiš	čísʲtʲət
(c)	'buy'	kupʲítʲ	kuplʲú	kúpʲiš	kúpʲət
	'draw lines'	grafʲítʲ	graflʲú	grafʲíš	grafʲát
	'catch'	lavʲítʲ	lavlʲú	lóvʲiš	lóvʲət
	'love'	lʲubʲítʲ	lʲublʲú	lʲúbʲiš	lʲúbʲət
	'introduce'	znakómʲitʲ	znakómlʲu	znakómʲiš	znakómʲət

(d) Classify the verbs according to shifts in stress. Is stress-shift predictable?
(e) Account for vowel alternations (see also Problem #32).

38. LATIN

Focus: endings and (primarily in the last two columns) stem-changes.
("pres." = present; "perf." = perfect; "pcp." = participle.)

		1. sg. pres.	infinitive	1. sg. perf.	pcp.
(a)	'write'	skri:bo:	skri:bere	skripsi:	skriptum
	'marry'	nu:bo:	nu:bere	nupsi:	nuptum
	'crawl'	re:po:	re:pere	repsi:	reptum
	'carve'	skulpo:	skulpere	skulpsi:	skulptum
(b)	'lead'	du:ko:	du:kere	duksi:	duktum
	'cook'	kokwo:	kokwere	koksi:	koktum
	'rule'	rego:	regere	reksi:	rektum
	'roast'	fri:go:	fri:gere	friksi:	friktum
	'join'	jungo:	jungere	junksi:	junktum
	'distinguish'	distingwo:	distingwere	distinksi:	distinktum
	'annoint'	ungwo:	ungwere	unksi:	unktum
	'look at'	spekjo:	spekere	speksi:	spektum
(c)	'shut'	klawdo:	klawdere	klawsi:	klawsum
	'bend'	flekto:	flektere	fleksi:	flektum
	'crush'	pinso:	pinsere	pinsi:	pinsum / pistum
	'shake'	kwatjo:	kwatere	kwassi:	kwassum
	'strike'	perkutjo:	perkutere	perkussi:	perkussum
	'send'	mitto:	mittere	mi:si:	missum
	'carry on'	gero:	gerere	gessi:	gestum
	'burn'	u:ro:	u:rere	ussi:	ustum
	'hurt'	lajdo:	lajdere	lajsi:	lajsum
	'retire'	ke:do:	ke:dere	kessi:	kessum
	'gnaw'	ro:do:	ro:dere	ro:si:	ro:sum
	'divide'	di:wido:	di:widere	di:wi:si:	di:wi:sum

CONTINUED→

Unit III

(38. LATIN, CONTINUED)

(d) 'take'	suːmoː	suːmere	sumpsiː	sumptum
'despise'	temnoː	temnere	tempsiː	temptum
'carry'	wehoː	wehere	weksiː	wektum
'draw'	trahoː	trahere	traksiː	traktum

39. TÜBATULABAL
   Focus: first, underlying stems; second, reason for variable vowel length in causative and benefactive suffixes.

		infinitive	imperfective	causative	benefactive
(a)	'eat'	tʌk	tʌkat	tʌkiːnat	tʌkaːnat
	'talk'	alaːw	alaːwat	alaːwinat	alaːwanat
	'see'	taːwʌk	taːwʌgat	taːwʌgiːnat	taːwʌgaːnat
	'get blisters'	pohol	poholat	poholiːnat	poholaːnat
	'do'	in	inʌt	iniːnat	inaːnat
	'sit'	halʔ	halʌt	haliːnat	halaːnat
	'get up'	oːl	oːlot	oːlinat	oːlanat
	'celebrate'	muːjh	muːhjut	muːhjinat	muːhjanat
	'pretend to eat'	tʌkiloːk	tʌkiloːgot	tʌkiloːginat	tʌkiloːganat
	'eat ravenously'	tʌkiwʌːt	tʌkiwʌːdʌt	tʌkiwʌːdinat	tʌkiwʌːdanat
	'make fast'	aːnaːlh	aːnaːhlʌt	aːnaːhlinat	aːnaːhlanat
	'play'	guːlʔ	guːlat	guːlinat	guːlanat
	'blow'	pušk	puškat	puškiːnat	puškaːnat
	'grow'	ajaːw	ajaːwʌt	ajaːwinat	ajaːwanat
	'boil'	moːnʔ	moːnot	moːninat	moːnanat
(b)	'arrive'	pʌlʌːla	pʌlʌːlat	pʌlʌːlinat	pʌlʌːlanat
	'hold'	jʌːwu	jʌːwut	jʌːwinat	jʌːwanat

40. HINDI-URDU
   Focus: the suffixes -õ: (oblique plural, m./f.), -ẽ: (direct plural, f.),
   -i:la: and -i: (adjectivizers), and their phonological effect when
   added to a noun stem.

(a)	'book'	kɪtaːb	kɪtaːbẽ	'thing'	ciːz	ciːzẽː
	'table'	meːz	meːzẽː	'eye'	ãːkʰ	ãːkʰẽː
	'army'	fɔːɟ	fɔːɟẽ	'buffalo'	bʰæ̃ːs	bʰæ̃ːsẽː
	'mill'	mɪl	mɪlẽː	'mosque'	mʌsʒiːd	mʌsʒiːdẽ
	'fruit'	pʰʌl	pʰʌlõː	'house'	mʌkaːn	mʌkaːnõː
	'ox'	bʰæːl	bʰæːlõː	'farmer'	kɪsaːn	kɪsaːnõː
(b)	'road'	sʌɽʌk	sʌɽkõː	'politics'	sɪjaːsʌt	sɪjaːstõː
	'mouth'	dɛhʌn	dɛhnõː	'worshiper'	puʒaːrʌn	puʒaːrnõː
	'city'	šɛhʌr	šɛhrõː	'invitation'	daːwʌt	daːwtõː
	'heaven'	fʌlʌk	fʌlkõː	'100 million'	ʌrʌb	ʌrbõː
	'glance'	nʌzʌr	nʌzrõː			
(c)	'woman'	ɔːrʌt	ɔːrtẽː	'shape'	suːrʌt	suːrtẽː
	'habit'	aːdʌt	aːdtẽː	'decoration'	sʌʒaːwʈ	sʌʒaːwʈẽː
	'meeting'	bæːʈʰʌk	bæːʈʰkẽː	'sister'	bʌhʌn	bʌhnẽː
	'crop'	fʌsʌl	fʌslẽː			
(d)	'tree'	dʌrʌxt	dʌrʌxtõː	'bed'	pʌlʌŋg	pʌlʌŋgõː
	'letter'	ʌkšʌr	ʌkšʌrõː	'book'	pustʌk	pustʌkẽː
(e)	'anklet'	ɟʰãːɟʰʌr	ɟʰãːɟʰʌrõː	'courtyard'	ãːgʌn	ãːgʌnõː
	'cricket'	ɟʰẽːgʌɽ	ɟʰẽːgʌɽõː	'ropemaker'	bʰãːʒʌk	bʰãːʒʌkõ
	'refreshments'	sãːbʰʌr	sãːbʰʌrõː			
(f)	'craze'	sʌnʌk	sʌnkiː	'brilliance'	cʌmʌk	cʌmkiːlaː
	'building'	iːmaːrʌt	iːmaːrti	'wickedness'	šʌraːrʌt	šʌraːrtiː
	'ostentation'	dɪkʰaːwʌʈ	dɪkʰaːwʈiː			

(g) What is the underlying vowel system of Hindi-Urdu?

Unit III

41. SUNDANESE
Focus: variation between root (first form given) and verb (second).

(a)	'buy'	boroŋ	ŋaboroŋ	'eat'	dahar	ŋadahar
	'answer'	ǰawab	ŋaǰawab	'change'	ganti	ŋaganti
	'dry skins'	widaŋ	ŋawidaŋ	'pass'	liwat	ŋaliwat
	'look after'	rawat	ŋarawat	'oppose'	mušuh	ŋamušuh
	'sadden'	nalaŋša	ŋanalaŋša	'make certain'	jakti	ŋajakti
	'inform'	ɲaho	ŋaɲaho	'work'	hanča	ŋahanča
	'take'	ʔala	ŋala	'drink'	ʔinum	ŋinum
(b)	'use'	pake	make	'beat'	tʏŋgʏl	nʏŋgʏl
	'think'	tenǰo	nenǰo	'take'	čokot	ɲokot
	'pursue'	šušul	ɲušul	'send'	kirim	ŋirim
(c)	'give'	bere	mere	'see'	dʏlʏ	nʏlʏ
	'make'	ǰiʏŋʏ	ɲiʏŋʏ	'bite'	gegel	ŋegel / ŋagegel
	'eat'	wadaŋ	madaŋ	'put in'	ʔasup	ŋasup / ŋaʔasup

42. GOTHIC
Focus: variation in the suffixes -iθa/-iða, -o:θus/-o:ðus, -uɸni/-uβni (all of which derive nouns from adjectives and verbs) and -axs/-aɣs (adjectivizer). (Note: inflectional endings in the simple form are separated from the stem by a hyphen.)

'deaf'	dawβ-s	dawβiθa	'mild'	mild-s	mildiθa
'foolish'	dwal-s	dwaliθa	'new'	niuj-is	niujiθa
'desert-like'	auθ-s	auθiða	'worthy'	wɛrθ-s	wɛrθiða
'famous'	me:r-s	me:riθa	'ready'	manw-us	manwiθa
'travel'	wrat-o:n	wrat-o:ðus	'human'	mannisk-s	mannisko:ðus
'mourn'	gaun-o:n	gauno:θus	'rule'	wald-an	walduɸni
'wounded'	wund-s	wunduɸni	'know'	wit-an	wituβni
'stone'	stain-s	stainaxs	'glory'	wulθ-us	wulθaɣs
'word'	wɔrd	wɔrdaxs			

43. HAUSA

Focus: tone, vowel, and consonant changes in verbs preceding pronoun and noun direct objects (note: [a] and [æ] are allophones of the same phoneme).

	verb	before pronoun	before noun
(a) 'change'	sáːkèː	sáːkèː	sáːkɛ̀
'count'	k'írgàː	k'írgàː	k'írgʌ̀
'release'	kwʌ́ɓèː	kwʌ́ɓèː	kwʌ́ɓɛ̀
'pay'	bíjǽː	bíjǽː	bíjɛ́
'see'	gʌ́níː	gʌ́níː	gʌ́ní
'read'	kʌ́Ɍʌntàː	kʌ́Ɍʌntàː	kʌ́Ɍʌntʌ̀
(b) 'look for'	nèːmáː	nèːméː	nèːmí
'ask about'	tʌ̀mbʌ́jǽː	tʌ̀mbʌ́jéː	tʌ̀mbʌ̀jí
'help'	tʌ̀jmʌ́kàː	tʌ̀jmʌ́kéː	tʌ̀jmʌ̀kí
'carry'	ɗʌ́wkàː	ɗʌ́wkéː	ɗʌ́wkí
'learn'	kòːjǽː	kòːjéː	kòːjí
'receive'	ʔʌ́msàː	ʔʌ́mšéː	ʔʌ́mší
'steal'	sàːtáː	sàːčéː	sàːčí
'cheat'	čùːtáː	čùːčéː	čùːčí
'buy'	sʌ̀jǽː	sʌ̀jéː	sʌ̀jí
'look (at)'	dúːbàː	dùːbéː	dùːbí

44. MODERN GREEK

Focus: stress patterns produced by adding, in (a), the enclitic possessives <u>mu</u> 'my', <u>mas</u> 'our', <u>tu</u> 'his', and, in (b), the enclitic object pronouns <u>me</u> 'me', <u>mu</u> 'to me', <u>to</u> 'it', <u>mas</u> 'us', <u>ti</u> 'her' to imperatives.

(a) 'brother'	aðerfós	aðerfós mu	'bill'	ɣramátio	ɣramátió mu
'car'	aftokínito	aftokínitó mu	'houses'	spítja	spítja mu
'chair'	karékla	karékla mas	'preference'	simpáθia	simpáθiá tu
'children'	peðí	peðí mu	'friend'	fílos	fílos tu
'book'	vivlío	vivlío mas	'man'	ánθropos	ánθropós mas
(b) 'give'	ðóse	ðóse mu		ðóse mú to	
'fix'	ðiórθose	ðiórθosé to		ðiórθosé mas to	
'send'	stíle	stíle to		stíle ti to	

Unit III

45. FINNISH
Focus: vowel harmony in case suffixes and (in (d)) stem variation. Key to cases: "nom." = nominative, "gen." = genitive, "par." = partitive, "ela." = elative, "tra." = translative, "all." = allative.

		nom.	gen.	par.	ela.	tra.	all.	nom. pl.
(a)	'school'	koulu	koulun	koulua	koulusta	kouluksi	koululle	koulut
	'train'	juna	junan	junaa	junasta	junaksi	junalle	junat
	'house'	talo	talon	taloa	talosta	taloksi	talolle	talot
(b)	'autumn'	syksy	syksyn	syksyæ	syksystæ	syksyksi	syksylle	syksyt
	'electricity'	sæhkø	sæhkøn	sæhkøæ	sæhkøstæ	sæhkøksi	sæhkølle	sæhkøt
	'cold'	kylmæ	kylmæn	kylmææ	kylm ææ	kylmæksi	kylmælle	kylmæt
(c)	'sleeve'	hiha	hihan	hihaa	hihasta	hihaksi	hihalle	hihat
	'row'	rivi	rivin	riviæ	rivistæ	riviksi	riville	rivit
	'victim'	uhri	uhrin	urhia	uhrista	uhriksi	uhrille	uhrit
	'door'	ovi	oven	ovea	ovesta	oveksi	ovelle	ovet
	'lake'	jærvi	jærven	jærveæ	jærvestæ	jærveksi	jærvelle	jærvet
	'nose'	nenæ	nenæn	nenææ	nenæstæ	nenæksi	nenælle	nenæt
(d)	'custom'	tapa	tavan	tapaa	tavasta	tavaksi	tavalle	tavat
	'weak'	heikko	heikon	heikkoa	heikosta	heikoksi	heikolle	heikot
	'ceiling'	laki	laen	lakea	laesta	laeksi	laelle	laet
	'boy'	poika	pojan	poikaa	pojasta	pojaksi	pojalle	pojat
	'end'	loppu	lopun	loppua	lopusta	lopuksi	lopulle	loput
	'meadow'	niitty	niityn	niittyæ	niitystæ	niityksi	niitylle	niityt
	'bird'	lintu	linnun	lintua	linnusta	linnuksi	linnulle	_____
	'comb'	kampa	kamman	kampaa	kammasta	kammaksi	kammale	_____
	'shoe'	keŋkæ	keŋŋæn	keŋkææ	keŋŋæstæ	keŋŋæksi	keŋŋælle	_____
	'bank'	paŋkki	paŋkin	paŋkkia	paŋkista	paŋkiksi	paŋkille	_____
	'field'	pelto	pellon	peltoa	pellosta	pelloksi	pellolle	_____
	'mother'	æiti	æidin	æitiæ	æidistæ	æidiksi	æidille	_____
	'ball'	pallo	pallon	palloa	pallosta	palloksi	pallolle	_____

46. HEBREW (ANCIENT)

Focus: variation in the form of the definite article prefix. (Accents = stress.)

			'the...'			'the...'
(a)	'road'	dérek	haddérek	'house'	bájit	habbájit
	'youth'	náʕar	hannáʕar	'king'	mélex	hammálex
	'door'	déleθ	haddéleθ	'field'	sá:ðeh	hassá:ðeh
	'corpse'	péɣer	happéɣer	'neighbor'	šá:xe:n	haššá:xe:n
(b)	'man'	ʔí:š	ha:ʔí:š	'stone'	ʔéven	ha:ʔéven
	'quarrel'	rí:v	ha:rí:v	'famine'	rá:ʕa:v	ha:rá:ʕa:v
	'city'	ʕí:r	ha:ʕí:r	'palace'	hé:xa:l	hahé:xa:l

47. POLISH

Focus: stem alternations. ("nom." = nominative, "acc." = accusative, "dat." = dative, "loc." = locative, "gen." = genitive. For the phonetic values and distinctive features of [ɕ] and [ʑ], see Introduction, Distinctive Features.

		nom. sg.	acc. sg.	dat./loc. sg.	gen. sg.
(a)	'porridge'	kaša	kaše	kašɪ	kašɪ
	'blackboard'	tablitsa	tablitse	tablitsɪ	tablitsɪ
	'kitchen'	kuxnʲa	kuxnʲe	kuxnʲi	kuxnʲi
	'beach'	plaža	plaže	plažɪ	plažɪ
	'shirt'	košula	košule	košuli	košuli
	'Sophia'	zofʲija	zofʲije	zofʲiji	zofʲiji
(b)	'fish'	rɪba	rɪbe	rɪbʲe	rɪbɪ
	'wardrobe'	šafa	šafe	šafʲe	šafɪ
	'grass'	trava	trave	travʲe	travɪ
	'winter'	ʑima	ʑime	ʑimʲe	ʑimɪ
	'skate'	wɪžva	wɪžve	wɪžvʲe	wɪžvɪ
	'foot'	stopa	stope	stopʲe	stopɪ

CONTINUED→

Unit III

(47. POLISH, CONTINUED)

(c)					
'river'	žeka	žeke	žetse	žekʲi
'book'	kɕõw̌ska	kɕõw̌ske	kɕõw̌stse	kɕõw̌skʲi
'blond'	blondɪnka	blondɪnke	blondɪntse	blondɪnkʲi
'leg'	noga	noge	nodẓe	nogʲi
'colleague'	kolega	kolege	koledẓe	kolegʲi
'fly'	muxa	muxe	muše	muxʲi
'newspaper'	gazeta	gazete	gazetɕe	gazetɪ
'post office'	počta	počte	počɕe	počtɪ
'desire'	oxota	oxote	oxotɕe	oxotɪ
'water'	voda	vode	vodẓe	vodɪ
'farm'	zagroda	zagrode	zagrodẓe	zagrodɪ
'Wednesday'	ɕroda	ɕrode	ɕrodẓe	ɕrodɪ
'sausage'	kʲewbasa	kʲewbase	kʲewbaɕe	kʲewbasɪ
'box office'	kasa	kase	kaɕe	kasɪ
'blouse'	bluza	bluze	bluẓe	bluzɪ
'visa'	vʲiza	vʲize	vʲiẓe	vʲizɪ
'wound'	rana	rane	ranʲe	ranɪ
'family'	rodẓina	rodẓine	rodẓinʲe	rodẓinɪ
'punishment'	kara	kare	kaže	karɪ
'cloud'	xmura	xmure	xmuže	xmurɪ
'school'	škowa	škowe	škole	škowɪ
'saw'	pʲiwa	pʲiwe	pʲile	pʲizɪ
'mother'	matka	matke	matse	matkʲi
'aunt'	tɕotka	tɕotke	tɕotse	tɕotkʲi
'opportunity'	šansa	_____	_____	_____
'goat'	koza	_____	_____	_____
'gauge'	mʲara	_____	_____	_____

48. WELSH
Focus: stem-initial variation when preceded by possessives.

		'her...'	'your...'	'his...'
'head'	pen	eifen	dəben	eiben
'father'	tad	eiθad	dədad	eidad
'money'	arjan	eiharjan	dəarjan	eiarjan
'tale'	hanes	eihanes	dəhanes	eihanes
'frankincense'	θɯs	eiθɯs	dəθɯs	eiθɯs
'ankle'	feːr	eifeːr	dəfeːr	eifeːr
'door'	porθ	eiforθ	dəborθ	eiborθ
'prudence'	kaɬineb	eixaɬineb	dəgaɬineb	eigaɬineb
'land'	tir	eiθir	dədir	eidir
'hand'	ɬaw	eiɬaw	dəlaw	eilaw
'intelligence'	deaɬ	eideaɬ	dəðeaɬ	eiðeaɬ
'brother'	brawd	eibrawd	dəvrawd	eivrawd
'anguish'	iŋ	eihiŋ	dəiŋ	eiiŋ
'zeal'	eiðgarux	eiheiðgarux	dəeiðgarux	eieiðgarux
'grandmother'	henvam	eihenvam	dəhenvam	eihenvam
'tooth'	dant	eidant	dəðant	eiðant
'garden'	garð	eigarð	dəarð	eiarð
'table'	bord	eibord	dəvord	eivord
'vicar'	viker	eiviker	dəviker	eiviker
'laughter'	xwerθin	eixwerθin	dəxwerθin	eixwerθin
'mouth'	keg	eixeg	dəgeg	eigeg

49. GERMAN

Focus: first, the consonantal alternations at the ends of stems in the singular and plural forms. Then proceed to vowel alternations in all forms; these are far more complex to formalize, especially the environment triggering the changes. Diminutive forms are abbreviated to conserve space; here, the stressed stem vowel is the one shown, the stem-final consonant is that in the singular form, and the suffix is variously [çən], [lajn], or [lɪŋ] (sometimes all three: 'little mouse' = [mɔʏsçən], [mɔʏslajn], [mɔʏslɪŋ]). Stress is on the first syllable, unless otherwise marked; r = [ʀ].

	sg.	pl.	feminine	diminutive	adjective	verb
'mouse'	maws	mɔʏzə		ɔʏ	mawzɪç	mawzən
'man'	man	mɛnər		ɛ	mɛnlɪç mɛnlɪš manhaft	
'day'	taːk	taːgə			tɛːklɪç	taːgən
'air'	lʊft	lʏftə		ʏ	lʏftlɪç	lʏftən
'country'	lant	lɛndər		ɛ	lɛntlɪç	landən
'calf'	kalp	kɛlbər	kalbə	ɛ		kalbən
'ball'	kuːgəl	kuːgəln		yː	kuːgəlɪç	kuːgəln
'grain'	kɔrn	kœrnər		œ	kœrnɪç	kœrnən
'head'	kɔpf	kœpfər		œ	kœpfɪç	kœpfən
'court'	hoːf	høːfə		øː	høːfɪš	
'ribbon'	bant	bɛndər		ɛ		
'bond'	bant	bandə				
'volume'	bant	bɛndə		ɛ	-bɛndɪç	
'God'	gɔt	gœtər	gœtɪn	œ	gœtlɪç	
'count'	graːf	graːfən	grɛːfɪn	ɛː	grɛːflɪç	
'doctor'	artst	ɛrtstə	ɛrtstɪn	ɛ	ɛrtstlɪç	
'dog'	hʊnt	hʊndə	hʏndɪn	ʏ	hʏndɪš	
'foot'	fuːs	fyːsə		yː	-fyːslɪç	
'point'	pʊŋkt	pʊŋktə		ʏ	pʏŋktlɪç	

CONTINUED→

(49. GERMAN, CONTINUED)

'person'	pɛrzóːn	pɛrzóːnən		øː	pɛrzǿːnlɪç	
'nature'	natúːr	natúːrən			natýːrlɪç	
'need'	noːt	nøːtə			nøːtɪç	nöːtən
'flea'	floː	catfløːə	catfløːɪn	øː		
'pressure'	drʊk	drʏkə				drʏkən
'print'	drʊk	drʊkə				drʊkən
'track'	špuːr	špuːrən			-špuːrɪç	špyːrən
'plan'	plaːn	plɛːnə		ɛː		plaːnən
'brother'	bruːdər	brÿːdər	(švɛstər)	yː	brÿːdərlɪç	
'hospital'	hɔspitáːl	hɔspitɛ́ːlər				
'wage'	loːn	løːnə				løːnən
'reward'	loːn	løːnə				loːnən
'fall'	fal	fɛlə				falən ('fall')
						fɛlən ('fell')
'hen'	huːn	hyːnər		yː		
'fool'	nar	narən	nɛrɪn	ɛ	nɛrɪš	narən
'metal'	metáːl	metáːlə			metáːlɪš	
'king'	køːnɪç	køːnɪgə	køːnɪgɪn		køːnɪklɪç	
'degree'	graːt	graːdə			graːduɛ́l	
'spice'	gəvÿrts	gəvÿrtsə			gəvÿrtsɪç	
'gas'	gaːs	gaːzə			gaːzɪç	
'prince'	fʏrst	fʏrstən	fʏrstɪn	ʏ	fʏrstlɪç	fʏrstən
'friend'	frɔʏnt	frɔʏndə	frɔʏndɪn	ɔʏ	frɔʏntlɪç	
'table'	tɪš	tɪšə		ɪ		
'sprout'	šprɔs	šprɔsə		œ		šprɔsən
'oil'	øːl	øːlə			øːlɪç	øːlən
'nerve'	nɛrf	nɛrvən			nɛrvǿːs	

(49. GERMAN, CONTINUED)

'bear'	bɛːr	bɛːrən	bɛːrɪn			
'tyrant'	tyrán	tyránən			tyránɪš	tyranizíːrən
'evening'	aːbənt	aːbəndə			aːbəntlɪç	
'spook'	špuːk	špuːkə		yː	špuːkhaft	špuːkən
'volcano'	vʊlkáːn	vʊlkáːnə			vʊlkáːnɪš	
'sheep'	šaːf	šaːfə			šaːfɪš	
'student'	študént	študéntən	študéntɪn		študéntɪš	
'type'	tyːp	tyːpən			tyːpɪš	
'push'	štoːs	štøːsə		øː	štøːsɪç	štoːsən
'peasant'	bawər	bawərn	bɔyərɪn	ɔч	bɔyərlɪç	
'armor'	harnɪš	harnɪšə				

50. ENGLISH (NON-STANDARD)
   Focus: final cluster simplification. Why does it occur in some cases but not in others? (Note: the actual outputs in (a) and (b) are more complex than indicated because the rule in question is variable. These data represent only general tendencies.)

(a)		(b)		(c)	
'sand'	sæn	'canned'	kʰænd	'card'	kʰard
'old'	oɫ	'rolled'	roɫd	'gulp'	gʌɫp
'told'	tʰoɫ	'filled'	fɪɫd	'jump'	ǰʌmp
'wind'	wɪn	'sinned'	sɪnd	'park'	pʰark
'best'	bɛs	'guessed'	gɛst	'belt'	bɛɫt
'wasp'	was	'slapped'	sɫæpt	'mint'	mɪnt
'fact'	fæk	'wrecked'	rɛkt	'dank'	dæŋk
'past'	pʰæs	'passed'	pʰæst	'harp'	harp
'product'	pradʌk	'ducked'	dʌkt	'pant'	pʰænt
'left'	ɫɛf				
'found'	fæwn				

51. SPANISH (AMERICAN)

Focus: each entry in (a) and (b) is shown with two forms, singular and plural. If the plural morpheme is /s/, then (a) has two solutions: (1) e-insertion in certain forms, or (2) e-deletion. Write up both solutions; given these data, either is adequate. Next, working on the basis of solution (2), determine why deletion is blocked in (b). Finally, consider the fate of English loanwords in colloquial Spanish. What global constraint holds in both (b) and (c)?

(a)
'blanket'	sarápe	sarápes		'glass'	báso	básos
'key'	ɟáβe	ɟáβes		'phone'	teléfono	teléfonos
'plum'	sirwéla	sirwélas		'chieftain'	kasíke	kasíkes
'victim'	bíktima	bíktimas		'tribe'	tríβu	tríβus
'shanty'	kasúča	kasúčas		'jail'	kársel	kárseles
'circle'	sírkulo	sírkulos		'guest'	wéspeð	wéspeðes
'stop'	paráða	paráðas		'root'	ŕais	ŕaíses
'garden'	xarðín	xarðínes		'truck'	kamjón	kamjónes
'sign'	seɲál	seɲáles		'woman'	muxér	muxéres
'pencil'	lápis	lápises		'policy'	pólisa	pólisas
'garage'	garáxe	garáxes		'angel'	áŋxel	áŋxeles
'virtue'	birtúð	birtúðes		'quake'	temblór	temblóres

(b)
'meat'	kárne	kárnes		'count'	kónde	kóndes
'sheriff'	alkálde	alkáldes		'multiple'	múltiple	múltiples
'post'	póste	póstes		'name'	nómbre	nómbres
'afternoon'	tárðe	tárðes		'gum'	číkle	číkles
'swan'	sízne	síznes		'candy'	dúlse	dúlses

(c)
record	→ ŕékor		lunch	→ lónče
standard	→ estándar		yard	→ ɟárða
yogurt	→ ɟoɣúr		tank	→ táŋke
zinc	→ sín		grant	→ grante
test	→ tés		rifle	→ ŕífle

Unit IV

Style and Dialect

1. SAMOAN
Focus: differences between formal and colloquial styles

	formal	colloquial		formal	colloquial
'cordyline'	tiː	kiː	'circle'	liʔo	liʔo
'valley'	vanu	vaŋu	'be true'	moni	moŋi
'key'	kiː	kiː	'uproot'	suati	suaki
'soldier'	fitafita	fikafika	'I'	sata	saka
'cave'	ana	aŋa	'boil'	saka	saka
'outrigger'	ama	ama	'mouth'	ŋutu	ŋuku
'span'	aŋa	aŋa	'strain'	ʔoʔono	ʔoʔoŋo

2. GERMAN
Focus: differences between formal (Style 1) and two informal styles.
Style 3, the most informal, differs from Style 2 only where indicated.
(Accents = stress.)

	1	2	3		1	2	3
'come'	kómən	kómm̩	kóm	'make use of'	nýtsən	nýtsn̩	
'give'	géːbən	géːbm̩	géːm	'sing'	zíŋən	zíŋŋ̩	zíŋ
'push'	šúpən	šúpm̩		'hack'	hákən	hákŋ̩	
'ripen'	ʀájfən	ʀájfm̩		'laugh'	láːxən	láːxŋ̩	
'hop'	hýpfən	hýpfm̩		'lie'	líːgən	líːgŋ̩	líːŋ
'run'	ʀénən	ʀénn̩		'fall'	fálən	fálən	
'talk'	ʀéːdən	ʀéːdn̩		'wish'	výnšən	výnšn̩	
'ride'	ʀájtən	ʀájtn̩		'reach'	ʀájçən	ʀájçn̩	
'tear'	ʀájsən	ʀájsn̩		'see'	zéːən	zéːn	
'travel'	ʀájzən	ʀájzn̩		'go'	géːən	géːn	
'hear'	hǿːʀən	hǿːʀən		'sow'	zɛ́ːən	zɛ́ːən	
'ask'	fʀáːgən	fʀáːgŋ̩	fʀáːŋ				

3. SPANISH (CASTILIAN)
Focus: differences between Style 1 (slow), Style 2 (colloquial educated), and Style (3) (popular). (Accents = stress.)

		1	2	3		1	2	3
(a)	'soldier'	soldáðo	soldáo	soldáw	'side'	láðo	láo	láw
	'lawyer'	aβoɣáðo	aβoɣáo	aβoɣáw	'cod'	bakaláo	bakaláo	bakaláw
(b)	'come'	beníðo	beníðo	beníw	'meal'	komíða	komíða	komía
	'served'	serβíðos	serβíðos	serβíws	'elbow'	kóðo	kóðo	kó:
(c)	'virtue'	birtúð	birtúθ	birtú	'come!'	beníð	beníθ	bení
	'lawn'	θéspeð	θéspeθ	θéspe	'truth'	berðáð	berðáθ	berðá
	'bring!'	traéð	traéθ	traé	'partridge'	perðíθ	perðíθ	perðíθ

4. GUJARATI
Focus: as above.

	1	2	3		1	2	3
'curse'	šap	sap	ħap	'snake'	sap	sap	ħap
'with a noose'	paše	pase	paħe	'nearby'	pase	pase	paħe
'rope'	kʌš	kʌs	kʌħ	'essence'	kʌs	kʌs	kʌħ
'dictionary'	koš	kos	koħ	'1.5 miles'	kos	kos	koħ
'station'	sṭešʌn	sṭesʌn	ħṭeħʌn	'what'	šũ	sũ	ħũ
'which (f.)'	ši	ši	ħi	'army'	lʌškʌr	lʌskʌr	lʌħkʌr
'boastfulness'	bʌr̭aš	bʌr̭as	bʌr̭aħ	'besides'	šiwaj	šiwaj	ħiwaj
'woman's dress'	sar̭i	sar̭i	ħar̭i	'which (m.)'	šo	so	ħo
'learning'	šikto	šikto	ħikto	'Russian'	ruši	ruši	ruħi
'pleasure'	sʌntoš	sʌntos	———	'lazy'	a̭lsu	a̭lsu	———
'eighty-one'	ikjasi	ikjaši	———	'cities'	šæhro	sæhro	———
'hunt'	šikar	———	———	'taxi'	ṭæksi		
'moved aside'	kʰʌsjo	kʰʌšjo	kʰʌħjo				

Unit IV   117

    5. FRENCH
       Focus: deletion and retention in colloquial French of the schwa in the
            clitics /kə/ 'that, it', /nə/ 'not', /tə/ 'you', /žə/ 'I', /mə/
            'me, myself', /lə/ 'it, him' /sə/ 'that, it, -self', /də/ 'of ---ing'
            (as in tired of ---ing); and, in (f), in the verbs /dəmãde/ 'ask for',
            /Rədəmãde/ 'ask for again'. The glosses are provided as rough labels
            only; meaning does not affect the behavior of /ə/ here.

(a) 'don't fall'   n tõbe pa   'don't sing'   n šãte pa

    'don't laugh'   n Rje pa   'don't move'   n buže pa

    'don't play'   n žwe pa   'to follow me'   m sɥive

    'to see it'   l vwaR   'to hide one-   s kaše
                                    self'

    'to do it'   l fɛR   'that price'   s pRi

(b) 'I read'   ž li   'I want'   ž vø

    'I respond'   ž Repõ   'I say'   ž di

    'I drink'   ž bwa   'I finish'   š fini

    'I can'   š pø   'I believe'   š kRwa

    'I know'   š sɛ   'I find'   š tRuv

(c) 'what is she   kə fɛt ɛl   'what is she   kə lit ɛl
       doing?'   reading?'
    'what does   kə dit ɛl   'what does   kə šãt ɛl
       she say?'   she sing?'
    'of reading'   də liR   'of finishing'   də finiR

    'of drinking'   də bwaR   'to prepare your   tə pRepaRe
                                  self'

    'to see you'   tə vwaR   'to tell you'   tə diR

(d) 'I find it'   žəl tRuv   'I see it'   žəl vwa

    'I don't know'   žən sɛ pa   'I don't read'   žən li pa

    'I believe it'   žəl kRwa   'to take it from me' məl pRãdR

    'it seems to me' səm sãbl   'it doesn't seem'   sən sãbl pa

    'to tell it to   səl diR   'of seeing it'   dəl vwaR
       oneself'
    'of seeing you'   dət vwaR   'of finding me'   dəm tRuve

    'I can't'   žən pø pa   'I wash myself'   žəm lav

                                                                                                        CONTINUED→

(5. FRENCH, CONTINUED)

(e)
'I say it to myself'	žəmlə di	'I don't believe you'	žəntə kʀwa pa
'don't tell it to me'	nəmlə di pa	'don't say it to yourself'	nətlə di pa
'of telling it to you'	dətlə diʀ	'that I would like it'	kəžlə vudʀe
'that I repeat it to myself'	kəžməl ʀepɛt	'I don't tell it to you'	žəntəl di pa

(f)
'I ask'	žə dmãd	'I ask for it'	žəl dəmãd
'I don't ask for it'	žənlə dmãd pa	'I don't ask for it again'	žənlə ʀdəmãd pa
'I ask for it again'	žəl ʀedmãd	'of asking it of oneself'	dəslə dmãde
'of asking you for it'	dətlə dmãde	'of asking you for it again'	dətlə ʀdəmãde

(g)
'I tell you'	štə di	'that which I tell you'	skə štə di
'I find you'	štə tʀuv	'that which I ask you for again'	skə štə ʀdəmãd
'I want you'	štə vø	'I say it to you'	štəl di
'I ask for you'	štə dmãd	'I ask you for it again'	štəl dəmãd

6. CHINESE (PEKING)
Focus: phonological consequences of change in tempo. (Raised numerals represent tonemes holding over the preceding syllable.)

		slow	fast		slow	fast
(a)	'isn't'	bu̥:²sr̥⁴	bu̥sr²	'thanks'	sie:⁴sie:⁴	siesi⁴
	'thumb'	dḁ⁴mezr³	dam⁴zr³	'buttocks'	pi⁴gu	pi⁴gu
(b)	'we'	ue³men²	uem³	'you (pl.)'	ni³men²	nim³
	'they'	ta¹men²	tam¹	'we (incl.)'	zan̥²men²	zam̥²
	'how much'	du̥e¹me	du̥em¹	'what'	sreme²	srem²
	'that way'	neme⁴	nem⁴	'how'	zeme³	z̥em³

Unit IV

7. SPANISH
Focus: variation in two Spanish dialects. Note: (h) represents variable aspiration which drops depending on style and social level.

		Castilian		Andalucian	
		sg.	pl.	sg.	pl.
(a)	'cough'	tós	tóses	tó(h)	tósɛ(h)
	'lily'	lís	líses	lí(h)	lísɛ(h)
	'mouth'	bóka	bókas	bóka	bɔ́kæ(h)
	'fist'	púɲo	púɲos	púɲo	púɲɔ(h)
	'pen'	plúma	plúmas	plúma	plúmæ(h)
	'house'	kása	kásas	kása	kásæ(h)
	'kiss'	béso	bésos	béso	bɛ́sɔ(h)
	'sun'	sól	sóles	sól	sɔ́lɛ(h)
	'step'	páso	pásos	páso	pásɔ(h)
	'end'	fín	fínes	fíŋ	fínɛ(h)
	'tooth'	djénte	djénte	djénte	djéntɛ(h)
	'temple'	sjén	sjénes	sjéŋ	sjénɛ(h)
	'tribe'	tríβu	tríβus	tríβu	tríβu(h)
	'match'	fósforo	fósforos	fófforo	fófforɔ(h)
	'stupid'	estúpiðo	estúpiðos	ɛttúpiðo	ɛttúpɪðɔ(h)
(b)	'the boot'	la βóta	laz βótas	la βóta	laɸɸɔ́tæ(h)
	'the drop'	la ɣóta	laz ɣótas	la ɣóta	laxxɔ́tæ(h)
	'the shower'	la ðúča	laz ðúčas	la ðúča	laθθúčæ(h)
	'the paw'	la páta	las pátas	la páta	lappátæ(h)
	'the cloth'	la téla	las télas	la téla	lattɛ́læ(h)
	'the tail'	la kóla	las kólas	la kóla	lakkɔ́læ(h)
	'the hand'	la máno	laz mános	la máno	lañmánɔ(h)
	'the grade'	la nóta	laz nótas	la nóta	lañnɔ́tæ(h)

8. ENGLISH
   Focus: phonetic manifestations of underlying /r/. Note that the phones represented by [ɜ ɚ ɹ ɻ ɘ] are quite similar, despite the different symbols.
   Key to forms: 1 = 1. sg. present;
   2 = 3. sg. present;
   3 = past;
   4 = gerund/present participle.

	General American				Standard British			
	1	**2**	**3**	**4**	**1**	**2**	**3**	**4**
(a) 'share'	šɛɻ̯	šɛɻ̯z	šɛɻ̯d	šɛɻ̯ʷɪŋ	šɛɘ̯	šɛɘ̯z	šɛɘ̯d	šɛɹɪŋ
'fear'	fɪɻ̯	fɪɻ̯z	fɪɻ̯d	fɪɻ̯ʷɪŋ	fɪɘ̯	fɪɘ̯z	fɪɘ̯d	fɪɹɪŋ
'roar'	ɻ̯ʷɔɻ̯	ɻ̯ʷɔɻ̯z	ɻ̯ʷɔɻ̯d	ɻ̯ʷɔɻ̯ʷɪŋ	ɹɔː	ɹɔːz	ɹɔːd	ɹɔːɹɪŋ
'lure'	luɻ̯	luɻ̯z	luɻ̯d	luɻ̯ʷɪŋ	luɘ̯	luɘ̯z	luɘ̯d	luɹɪŋ
'bar'	baɻ̯	baɻ̯z	baɻ̯d	baɻ̯ʷɪŋ	baː	baːz	baːd	baɹɪŋ
'prefer'	pɻ̯ʷɪfɚ	pɻ̯ʷɪfɚz	pɻ̯ʷɪfɚd	pɻ̯ʷɪfɚɻ̯ʷɪŋ	pɹɪfɜː	pɹɪfɜːz	pɹɪfɜːd	pɹɪfɜːɹɪŋ

(b) Cockney has essentially the same values for the above six words as Standard British. Extend your analysis to include the additional Cockney data shown below.

'roll'	ɹow	ɹowz	ɹowd	ɹoɫɪn
'fill'	fïɰ	fïɰz	fïɰd	fïɫɪn
'pull'	pʊw	pʊwz	pʊwd	pʊɫɪn
'lull'	ɫʌɰ	ɫʌɰz	ɫʌɰd	ɫʌɫɪn
'spell'	spɛ̈ɰ	spɛ̈ɰz	spɛ̈ɰd	spɛ̈ɫɪn
'snarl'	snäɰ	snäɰz	snäɰd	snäɫɪn

Unit IV   121

9. GERMAN
   Focus: Standard German [g] and [ŋ] and equivalents in North German.
          (Cf. also Unit III, #1 and #49.)

		Std. Ger.	N. Ger.		Std. Ger.	N. Ger.
(a)	'smuggle'	šmugəln	šmuɣəln	'rain'	ʀeːgən	ʀeːɟən
	'ensign'	flagə	flaɣə	'gypsy'	tsigɔynəʀ	tsiɟɔynəʀ
	'bend'	biːgən	biːɟən	'lie'	lyːgən	lyːɟən
	'govern'	ʀegiːʀən	ʀeɟiːʀən	'bow'	boːgən	boːɣən
	'hesitate'	tsøːgəʀn	tsøːɟəʀn	'fig'	fajgə	fajɟə
	'good'	guːt	ɟuːt	'God'	gɔt	ɟɔt

		Std. Ger.		N. Ger.	
		sg.	pl.	sg.	pl.
(b)	'day'	taːk	taːgə	taːx	taːɣə
	'victory'	ziːk	ziːgə	ziːç	ziːɟə
	'flight'	fluːk	flyːgə	fluːx	flyːɟə
	'curse'	fluːx	flyːçə	fluːx	flyːçə
	'dock'	dɔk	dɔkə	dɔk	dɔkə
	'clever' ('hole')	lɔx	lœçəʀ	lɔx	lœçəʀ
	'strong'	štaʀk	štaʀkə	štaʀk	štaʀkə
	'coffin'	zaʀk	zɛʀgə	zaʀç	zɛʀɟə
	'bird'	foːgəl	føːgəl	foːɣəl	føːɟəl
	'road'	veːk	veːgə	veːç	veːɟə
	'husk'	balk	bɛlgə	balç	bɛlɟə
(c)	'thing'	dɪŋ	dɪŋəʀ	dɪŋk	dɪŋəʀ
	'hope'	hɔfnuŋ	hɔfnuŋən	hɔfnuŋk	hɔfnuŋən
	'seaweed'	taŋ	taŋə	taŋk	taŋə
	'tank'	taŋk	taŋkə	taŋk	taŋkə
	'finger'	fɪŋəʀ	fɪŋəʀ	fɪŋəʀ	fɪŋəʀ

10. ENGLISH

Focus: fronting, lowering, backing, rounding, and glide deletion in the diphthongs /aj/ and /aw/; you may assume these as the underlying representations. The values for side are also those of five, mile size, lie, nine; for twice, also those of knife, sight, like; for down, also those of loud, blouse, gouge, cow; for out, also those of mouth, house, couch, mouse. For simplicity, you may ignore the front/back difference between [aˈ] and [aˈ] and concentrate on that between these two and [æ]. However, outside of this problem the difference is significant in that the side [saˈd] of Dialects 6-10 contrasts (on the phonetic surface) with both sod [saˈd] and sad [sæd].

	SIDE	TWICE	DOWN	OUT
1. Rochester (N. Y.) and Std. British	aˈj	aˈj	aˈw	aˈw
2. Charleston (S. C.) and Ontario	aˈj	ɐj	aˈw	ɐw
3. Harrisburg (Pa.)	aˈj	aˈj	æw	æw
4. Northeastern North Carolina	aˈj	ɐj	æw	æw
5. Winchester (Va.)	aˈj	ɐj	æw	ɐw
6. ⎫ Central North Carolina	aˈ	aˈ	æw	æw
7. ⎭	aˈ	aˈj	æw	æw
8. Richmond and Petersburg (Va.)	aˈ	ɐj	æw	ɐw
9. Roanoke (Va.)	aˈ	aˈj	æw	ɐw
10. Savannah (Ga.)	aˈ	ɐj	aˈw	ɐw
11. Baltimore (Md.)	aˈj	aˈj	æw	ɐw
12. Cockney	ɒj	ɒj	εw	εw
13. Birmingham (U. K.)	ɔj	ɔj	aˈw	aˈw
14. Somerset (U. K.)	ɜj	ɜj	εɥ	εɥ

Sources

Abaev, V. I., A Grammatical Sketch of Ossetic (transl. by Steven Hill), Bloomington, Ind.: Indiana University Press, 1964.
Alonso, Dámaso, Alonso Zamora Vicente, María Josefa Canellada de Zamora, "Vocales andaluzas," Nueva Revista de Filología Hispánica 4:209-230, 1950.
Arauz, Próspero, El Pipil de la región de los itzalcos, San Salvador: Ministerio de Cultura, 1960.
Armstrong, Lilias E., The Phonetic and Tonal Structure of Kikuyu, London: Dawsons, 1940.
Arnott, D. W., The Nominal and Verbal Systems of Fula, Oxford: Clarendon Press, 1970.
Badia Margarit, Antonio, Gramática catalana, Madrid: Editorial Gredos, 1962.
Beeler, M. S., "Sibilant Harmony in Chumash," IJAL 36:14-17, 1970.
Bills, Graland, Bernardo Vallejo, Rudolph Troike, An Introduction to Spoken Quechua, Austin: University of Texas Press, 1969.
Cardona, George, A Gujarati Reference Grammar, Philadelphia: University of Pennsylvania Press, 1965.
Cole, Desmond and Dingaan Mpho Mokaila, A Course in Tswana, Washington: Georgetown University, 1962.
Delattre, Pierre, Les difficultés phonétiques du français, Middlebury College, 1948.
Dirks, Sylvester, "Campa (Arawak) Phonemes," IJAL 19:302-304, 1953.
Dixon, R. M. W., The Dyirbal Language of North Queensland, Cambridge: Cambridge University Press, 1972.
Doke, Clement, Phonetics of the Zulu Language (Bantu Studies II), Johannesburg: University of the Witwatersrand Press, 1926.
Echeverría, Max and Heles Contreras, "Araucanian Phonemics," IJAL 31:132-135, 1965.
Elson, Benjamin F. (ed.), Phonemic Systems of Colombian Languages, Summer Institute of Linguistics, Norman, Okla.: University of Oklahoma Press, 1967.
Elson, Benjamin F. (ed.), Studies in Peruvian Indian Languages, I, Summer Institute of Linguistics, Norman, Okla.: University of Oklahoma Press, 1963.
Evans, H. M. and W. O. Thomas, Y Geiriadur Newydd: The New Welsh Dictionary, Llandebie: Llyfrau'r Dryw, 1953.
Firestone, Homer, "Chama Phonology," IJAL 21:52-55, 1955.
Firestone, Homer, Description and Classification of Siriono, The Hague: Mouton, 1965.
Fortune, G., An Analytical Grammar of Shona, London: Longmans, Green & Co., 1955.
Gibson, Lorna, "Pame (Otomí) Phonemics and Morphophonemics," IJAL 22:242-265, 1956.
Gordon, E. V., An Introduction to Old Norse, London: Oxford University Press, 1927.
Hall, Robert A., jr. Hungarian Grammar, supplement to Language 20, 1944.
Hockett, Charles F., "Peiping Morphophonemics," Language 26:63-85, 1950.
Hodge, Carleton T. and Ibrahim Umaru, Hausa: Basic Course, Washington: Foreign Service Institute, 1963.
Hoffman, Carl, A Grammar of the Margi Language, London: Oxford University Press, 1963.
Kraft, Charles H. and Marguerite G., Introductory Hausa, Berkeley: University of California Press, 1973.
Kurath, Hans and Raven McDavid, The Pronunciation of English in the Atlantic States, Ann Arbor: University of Michigan Press, 1961.
Lambdin, Thomas O., Introduction to Biblical Hebrew, New York: Scribner's, 1971.
Langdon, Margaret, "Metathesis in Yuman Languages," Language 52:866-883, 1976.
Lewis, G. L., Turkish Grammar, Oxford: Clarendon Press, 1967.
Lukas, Johannes, A Study of the Kanuri Language: Grammar and Vocabulary, London: Oxford University Press, 1937.
McArthur, Harry and Lucille, "Aguacatec (Mayan) Phonemes within the Stress Group," IJAL 22:72-76, 1956.
Maltzoff, Nocholas, Russian Reference Grammar, New York: Pitman, 1965.
Mason, J. Alden, The Language of the Papago of Arizona, Philadelphia: University of Pennsylvania Press, 1950.

Mikula, Bohumil, *Progressive Czech*, West, Tex.: Czechoslovak Publishing Co., 1936.
Moulton, W. G., *The Sounds of English and German*, Chicago: University of Chicago Press, 1962.
Milner, B. B., *Samoan Dictionary*, London: Oxford University Press, 1966.
Narang, G. C. and Donald A. Becker, "Aspiration and Nasalization in the Generative Phonology of Hindi-Urdu," *Language* 47:646-667, 1971.
Nasr, Raja T., *Colloquial Arabic*, Beirut: Systeco, 1966.
Navarro, Tomas, *Manual de pronunciación española*, New York: Hafner Publishing Co., 1967.
Oblensky, Serge, Debebow Zelelie, and Mulugeta Andualem, *Amharic: Basic Course*, Washington: Foreign Service Institute, 1964.
O'Connor, J. D., *Phonetics*, Middlesex, U. K.: Penguin, 1973.
Olli, John B., *Fundamentals of Finnish Grammar*, New York: Northland Press, 1958.
Olmsted, D. L., "Atsugewi Phonology," *IJAL* 24:215-220, 1958.
Painter, Colin, *Gonja: A Phonological and Grammatical Study*, Bloomington: Indiana University Press, 1970.
Park, B. Nam, *Korean--Basic Course*, Washington: Foreign Service Institute, 1968.
Polomé, E., *Swahili Language Handbook*, Washington: Center for Applied Linguistics, 1967.
Reed, Carroll E., *The Pennsylvania German Dialect Spoken in the Counties of Lehigh and Berks*, Seattle: University of Washington Press, 1949.
Robins, R. H., "The Phonology of the Nasalized Verbal Forms in Sundanese," *Bulletin of the School of Oriental and African Studies* 15:138-145, 1953.
Ruhlen, Merritt, *A Guide to the Languages of the World*, Stanford University, Language Universals Project, 1976.
Saib, Jilali, "Gemination and Spirantization in Berber," *Studies in African Linguistics* 5:1-26, 1974.
Schachter, Paul and F. T. Otanes, *Tagalog Reference Grammar*, Berkeley: University of California Press, 1972.
Schenker, Alexander M., *Beginning Polish*, New Haven: Yale University Press, 1973.
Smyth, H. W., *Greek Grammar* (revised by Gordon M. Messing), Cambridge, Mass.: Harvard University Press, 1968 (1920).
Stilman, Galina and William E. Harkins, *Introductory Russian Grammar*, Waltham, Mass.: Blaisdell, 1964.
Swadesh, Morris and Charles Voegelin, "A Problem in Phonological Alternation," *Language* 15:1-10, 1939.
Taylor, Douglas, "A Preliminary View of Arawak Phonology," *IJAL* 35:234-238, 1969.
Walker, Willard, "Toward the Sound Pattern of Zuni," *IJAL* 38:240-259, 1972.
Warburton, Irene P., *On the Verb in Modern Greek*, Bloomington: Indiana University Press, 1970.
Whitley, M. Stanley, *Toward a Generative Theory of Dialectology, with Reference to English, Scots, Spanish, and German Dialect Areas*, Cornell University PhD. dissertation, 1974.
Wonderley, William, "Zoque II: Phonemes and Morphophonemes," *IJAL* 17:105-123, 1951.
Wright, William, *Grammar of the Gothic Language* (revised by O. L. Sayce), London: Oxford University Press, 1972 (1910).

Index of Languages

Numbers refer to Unit and Exercise numbers, respectively.

Abkhazian: I-2
Aguacatec: II-5
Aleut: I-2
Amharic: II-8
Arabela: II-15
Arabic: I-7
Araucanian: II-31
Arawak: II-9
Atsugewi: II-26
Basque: I-2
Campa: I-2, II-19
Cantonese: I-2
Catalan: II-12, II-20, III-16
Chama: II-27
Cherokee: I-2
Chumash: I-6
Czech: I-8
Daga: II-2
Danish: I-2
Dutch: III-2, III-14
Dyirbal: III-19
English: II-36, III-50, IV-8, IV-10
Ewe: I-2
Fante: I-2
Finnish: III-45
French: II-10, III-17, III-26, IV-5
Fula: III-23
German: III-1, III-21, III-30, III-49, IV-2, IV-9
Gonja: II-23
Gothic: III-42
Greek: II-38, III-8, III-44
Gujarati: IV-4
Hausa: II-21, III-43
Hawaiian: I-2
Hebrew: I-2, III-46
Hindi: I-10, III-40
Italian: II-1, III-36
Japanese: II-37, III-35
Kanakanabu: I-2
Kanuri: III-27
Kikuyu: III-25
Kirghiz: I-2
Korean: II-23

Latin: III-7, III-38
Logbara: III-24
Magyar (Hungarian): III-18
Mandarin (Chinese): I-2, IV-6
Margi: II-34, III-20
Masai: I-2
Mohave: III-28
Mwera: III-11
Old Norse: II-24, II-35, III-31
Ossetic: II-3
Pame (Otomí): III-15
Papago: II-6
Pennsylvania German: II-14
Persian: I-2
Pipil: II-13
Polish: III-47
Portuguese: Introduction, I-2, III-5
Quechua: II-28
Rumanian: III-9
Russian: II-4, III-32, III-37
Salishan: I-2
Samoan: III-6, IV-1
Scots: II-29
Shona: III-3
Siriono: II-22
Spanish: Introduction, I-9, II-16, II-32, III-12, III-22, III-51, IV-3, IV-7
Suena: I-2
Sundanese: III-41
Swahili: I-2, II-25, III-13
Swedish: I-2
Tagalog: I-5, II-18
Tamazight: III-29
Tswana: II-11
Tübatulabal: III-39
Tucano: II-17
Turkish: I-2, III-34
Vietnamese: I-2
Welsh: I-2, III-48
Yakut: I-2
Yukaghir: I-2
Zoque: III-10
Zulu: II-7, III-33
Zuñi: II-30